MICROSOFT OFFICE 365 10 IN 1 2023 GUIDE FOR BEGINNERS

ANGEALE HAIMELTUN

INTRODUCTION

Welcome to the world of digital proficiency with the "Microsoft Office 365 10 in 1 2023 Guide for Beginners." This book is a comprehensive and detailed guide designed to help you understand and navigate the intricate features of Microsoft Office 365. The aim of this guide is to transform your basic knowledge about the suite into advanced expertise that will make you a proficient user of the Microsoft Office 365 suite. Whether you are a student, a business professional, a teacher, a researcher, or a freelancer, this guide is the perfect companion to help you understand and efficiently use the suite for your day-to-day tasks.

Microsoft Office 365 is a powerful, versatile, and reliable productivity suite that contains an array of tools, each designed to facilitate a specific function or set of functions. This suite comprises of Word, Excel, PowerPoint, OneNote, Access, Outlook, Teams, Publisher, OneDrive, and SharePoint. As a novice, you may find this suite daunting due to its wide range of applications and their specific features. This guide will simplify and make accessible the operations of each application, providing step-by-step instructions and offering tips and tricks to get the most out of Microsoft Office 365.

To ensure a smooth learning experience, we will start with the basics: getting started with Microsoft Office 365, exploring what it includes, its costs, installation options, and how to make the best purchase decision. We will also dive into OneDrive and its personal vault, an essential part of the suite that allows you to store and access your files securely.

As we move further, we'll delve into the individual applications starting with Microsoft Word. You'll learn about the interface, how to navigate using the menu bar, using different tabs, and the features and functions each tab offers.

In Part 2, we'll explore Excel, an indispensable tool for individuals and businesses alike. This section will acquaint you with Excel's user interface, file formats, and the concepts of spreadsheets, cells, rows, and columns. We will also discuss some of the real-world applications of Excel in various sectors.

Next, we focus on PowerPoint, a powerful presentation tool that helps you convey your ideas effectively. Here, we will walk you through creating presentations from preset templates and familiarize you with the user interface.

The subsequent sections will introduce you to OneNote, Access, Outlook, Teams, Publisher, OneDrive, and SharePoint. For each application, we will discuss the basics, unique features, and practical tips to enhance your productivity.

With Access, you will learn about database management and key terminologies. In Outlook, you will understand email management, search features, and category creation. As for Teams, you will grasp the art of online collaboration and communication. With Publisher, we will cover publication creation and troubleshooting common Office 365 issues. In OneDrive, we focus on setting up an account, sharing files, and managing your files efficiently. Lastly, in SharePoint, you'll learn about site creation, content management, and how to optimize your SharePoint experience.

A crucial part of the guide is the emphasis on troubleshooting common issues. We aim to empower you not just to use, but to manage and maintain the applications independently. We will guide you through common challenges and solutions, preparing you to face any issue that may arise during your Office 365 experience.

This guide also pays attention to making the learning process user-friendly. We've employed simple language, relatable examples, and well-structured instructions to facilitate understanding. The content is arranged progressively, so you understand each part before moving to the next, ensuring a comprehensive grasp of the suite.

It is important to note that mastery does not come overnight. It requires patience, practice, and persistence. Microsoft Office 365 is a powerful suite that offers a multitude of features that can substantially improve your productivity when utilized effectively. This guide is a valuable resource, but the onus is on you to practice and explore the suite. Be ready to make mistakes and learn from them. That's the most effective way to grow your skills and capabilities.

As we progress through the book, we will also focus on some lesser-known but valuable tips and shortcuts. These gems will enhance your productivity and make the suite more enjoyable to use.

One of the unique features of this guide is its holistic approach to the Microsoft Office 365 suite. Often, users get comfortable with one or two applications, missing out on the incredible benefits the other applications offer. This guide encourages you to break out of your comfort zone and explore the entire suite. You may be surprised to find that an application you've been ignoring can significantly improve your work efficiency or provide solutions to issues you've been facing.

Furthermore, Microsoft Office 365 is a cloud-based suite, which means you can access your work from anywhere, at any time, and on any device. We will explore this feature in depth, ensuring that you can leverage the flexibility and accessibility it offers.

This guide is not just about learning; it's about building confidence in using the Microsoft Office 365 suite. We will ensure that by the end of this book, you are not just familiar with the suite, but are comfortable using it for various tasks. Whether you need to draft a document, make a presentation, manage a database, organize your emails, work collaboratively, or design a publication, you'll be equipped with the knowledge and skills to do so efficiently.

It's important to remember that Microsoft Office 365 is constantly evolving. While this guide is based on the 2023 version of the suite, Microsoft frequently releases updates to improve features and functions. To stay updated and get the most from the suite, it's advisable to keep an eye on these updates and explore them as they arrive.

In conclusion, this guide will be your navigator, mentor, and companion in your journey to Microsoft Office 365 proficiency. We believe that with this book by your side, you'll be well-equipped to make the most of this productivity suite and take your skills to the next level.

As we embark on this exciting journey together, keep in mind the words of the philosopher Confucius, "I hear and I forget. I see and I remember. I do and I understand." It's not enough to read this guide; practice as much as possible. It's through doing that we truly understand.

Get ready to dive in, explore, learn, and transform your digital productivity with the Microsoft Office 365 10 in 1 2023 Guide for Beginners! Happy learning!

CONTENTS

Getting Started

Microsoft Office 365 is a subscription-based suite of business applications. It could be the solution you're looking for if you need to upgrade your business software or want to try something new. This article will explain everything you need to know about Microsoft Office 365, including how it works and what it offers. We'll also tell you how much it costs and some of its key features so that you can decide if this service is right for your business.

Microsoft Office 365 is a subscription-based software suite that includes the full Microsoft Office applications, including Word, Excel, PowerPoint, Outlook, and Access. The cloud version of these applications is hosted on Microsoft's servers and allows users to access them from anywhere at any time via a browser or mobile device.

Microsoft 365 also includes other Microsoft applications and services such as OneDrive for Business (cloud storage), Skype for Business (online meetings and collaboration), and Windows Defender Antivirus.

Microsoft Office 365 is a subscription-based product. You pay a monthly or annual fee and get all the latest Word, Excel, PowerPoint, Outlook, and more versions. Microsoft Office 365 offers some benefits over traditional versions of these applications:

- It's easy to install Office on multiple devices (including Macs), so you can work where you're most comfortable.

- Each person gets 1 TB of OneDrive storage for storing files in the cloud—you'll never run out of space!

- The premium version includes additional features such as access to Power BI (business intelligence), advanced analytics tools for data science professionals; Access database software; Skype for Business Online conferencing capabilities; Yammer enterprise social network software; Delve shared inbox search app built into Outlook that helps users discover what others are working on inside your organization's network without leaving their inboxes behind

; and Office 365 Groups, which allows users to collaborate with others in the same group. The basic version of Office 365 includes Word, Excel, and PowerPoint with limited functionality; the premium version includes additional features such as access to Power BI (business intelligence), advanced analytics tools for data science professionals; Access to database software; Skype for

Business Online conferencing capabilities; Yammer enterprise social network software

Office 365, the premium version of Microsoft Office, comes with more features than the classic version. There are several different versions of Office 365 that you can choose from, depending on your needs:

- The Business Premium plan includes Office 365 (desktop apps), Exchange Online (email hosting), SharePoint Online (file sharing and collaboration), Skype for Business Online (online meetings and messaging), and OneDrive for Business (cloud storage). This plan allows up to five users access to these applications at once.

- The Enterprise E1 plan includes all the benefits of the Business Premium plan but also adds Security & Compliance Center monitoring tools, Identity Protection service for $4 per user per month or $30 per user annually — plus other services like Advanced Threat Analytics or Endpoint Protection Service.

How many devices can we install Office on?

Office 365 is available for one PC or Mac, tablet, and phone, and it can be installed on up to five devices (for example, you could install it on your work computer, laptop, and smartphone). You can also install Office 365 on the PC or Mac you use at home if you already have an existing subscription.

Office 365 is available for up to five users per subscription (so five people can use it together)

Microsoft 365 includes 1 TB of OneDrive

OneDrive is a cloud-based storage service that allows you to store files, photos, and videos in the cloud. It's accessible from any device connected to the internet, allowing you to access your files anywhere at any time. With 1 TB of storage space on OneDrive Personal Vault, you can upload all of your important files without worrying about running out of space.

While 1 TB may seem like an overwhelming amount of space—and it is!—it's still necessary for some users to pay for more than 2TB (for example, people who work with high-resolution images). Several options are available for these people, including Office 365 Business Essentials, which includes 3TB for just $10 per month per user, and Office 365 Business Premium, which includes 5TB for $12 per month per user. The subscription plan will also include other benefits such as security software such as Windows Defender Advanced Threat Protection or Advanced Threat Analytics service that helps identify advanced threats through data collection analysis and collaboration tools like Planner or

Yammer so teams can stay connected on projects without having to waste time setting up meetings in Outlook calendar (or worse yet face-to-face).

What is OneDrive's Personal Vault?

OneDrive Personal Vault is the newest feature in OneDrive, Microsoft's cloud storage service. It's designed to provide you with protection for your most important files and folders. OneDrive Personal Vault will help you organize and secure your most sensitive documents and make them available on all your devices whenever you need them, even offline.

OneDrive Personal Vault will be available soon; sign up now to get early access and be among the first to try it out!

Even more premium apps with Microsoft 365

Microsoft 365 is the best way to access the full breadth of Microsoft Office applications. It includes:

- OneNote – An app for taking notes, creating lists, and annotating webpages

- PowerPoint – Create beautiful presentations with this software tool

- Word – Save your ideas in a document or create a newsletter, letter, or report

- Outlook – Manage your email and organize contacts with this email application

- Excel – Perform complex calculations on large amounts of data with Excel. Also, create graphs and charts to visualize large quantities of information

- Publisher - Design newsletters, publications, and other materials using Publisher. It's easy to customize them using templates or by editing the text directly in the application

- Access - Access lets you build databases that can be accessed easily by multiple people at once (if they have access)

How much does Microsoft 365 cost?

The cost of Microsoft 365 depends on which version you choose, but they all fall into similar price ranges. The most basic version, Microsoft 365 Business, is $12.50 per user per month; the middle option, Microsoft 365 Enterprise E3, costs $20.83 per user per month; and the highest-end version—Microsoft 365 Enterprise E5—costs $27.16 per user per month (prices may vary in your area). Other versions of the software range from $32.50 to $41 a year for an individual license or between 10 and 15 times that for a business license for up to 5 users ($250-$375).

How to save money on the purchase of Microsoft 365 Family or Personal?

- Microsoft 365 offers a 25% discount for students and teachers.

- Microsoft 365 offers a 15% discount for government employees and non-profit organizations.

- Microsoft 365 offers a 10% discount to those who have an active Office 365 subscription (this is automatically applied).

What about Microsoft technical support?

Microsoft 365 technical support is available 24/7. If you need help with your Office 365 subscription, you can contact Microsoft support by phone, chat, or email. You can also contact Microsoft support via Twitter.

Microsoft 365 technical support is available in multiple languages and supports all versions of Microsoft 365: Business, Enterprise E3, E5, and Education.

You can motivate yourself without being mean to yourself.

You can motivate yourself without being mean to yourself.

How? It all starts with self-compassion: your ability to be kind and compassionate toward yourself in the face of failure, disappointment, or other life challenges.

In this article, we'll talk about why being kind to yourself is important and how you can do that even more effectively when you don't have time for a lengthy meditation session (like right after you mess up at work).

Book 1: - Word

Word 365 is a word processing tool included in Microsoft's Office 365 line of subscription services that lets users create documents and reports of a professional grade. A web browser that is already installed on the computer can be used to provide letters and resumes in more depth online. Word 365, also called Word Online, only works with web browsers on computers and saves files to the cloud.

Word 365: Word 365 was introduced on September 24, 2011, along with the other products in the Office 365 lineup of subscription services offered by Microsoft, to let users create documents and reports at a professional level. A web browser that is already installed on the computer can be used to provide letters and resumes in more depth online. This edition of Word comes with features like vocal dictation, resume assistant, and online document sharing, among others.

Exploring Word 365 Screen Interface

Word 365 has the same screen interface as the traditional Word (2010, 2013, 2016, and 2019). The only difference here is that; Word 365 is used within the web browser.

Here in this session, we will explain the features of Word 365. These features will be based on the Title bar and the Menu bar.

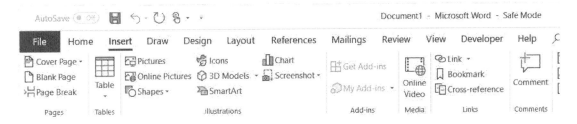

The Title Bar

The name of the currently being worked-on document is shown in the Title bar. The top of the screen interface is where you'll find the Title bar. As seen in the screenshot below, the document's name, such as Document 1, is displayed at the top of the screen.

Utilizing the Menu Bar to Navigate

The Title bar is immediately followed by the Menu bar. The tabs required to use Word 365 are all located in the Menu bar. The file is the first tab on the menu bar, and Help is the last.

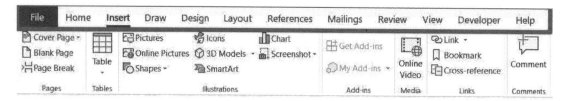

Let's examine each tab on the menu bar to see what it does and how it is used.

File Tab

The File tab is the first to see when you go to the Menu bar. When you click on the File tab, the following features are displayed

- **Home:** When you click on Home under the File tab, you get to see the following features
  - **New:** This option allows you to open a new document.
  - **Open:** This option allows you to open a previously saved document.

- **Info:** This option offers extra details about the document you've worked on, including its size, words, pages, the total number of edits, title, tags, and other details. This option can safeguard your work, limit modification, and look for problems.

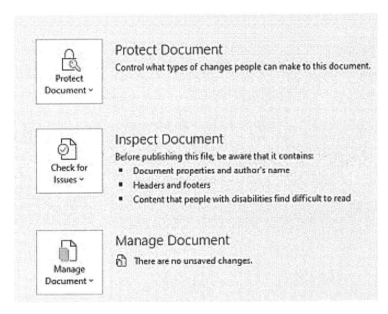

- **Save:** This option allows you to save the active document with its current file name, location, and format.

- **Save As:** You can use this option to save the currently open document with its current location, file name, and format.

Save As

Save As
Save a copy online.

Rename
Rename this file.

Download a Copy
Download a copy to your computer.

Download as PDF
Download a copy of this document to your computer as a PDF file.

Download as ODT
Download a copy of this document to your computer as an ODT file.

Where's the Save Button?

There's no Save button because we're automatically saving your document.

- **Print:** You can print the active settings and modify them using this option.

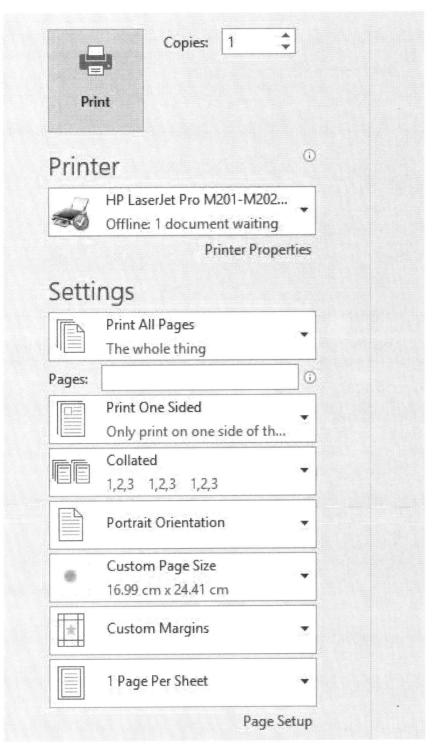

- **Share:** You have the choice to use this to share your documents with others online via blogs, websites, or emails.

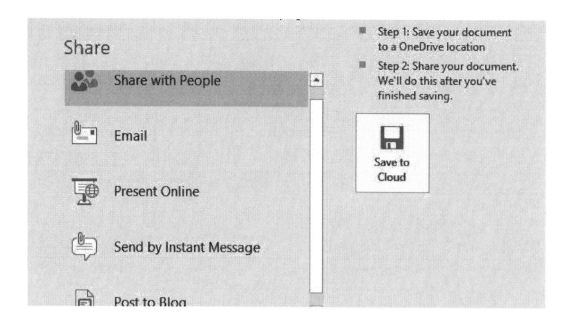

- **Export:** By altering the file formats, you can use the Export option to move a file from Word into another Office 365 application, such as PowerPoint or Excel.

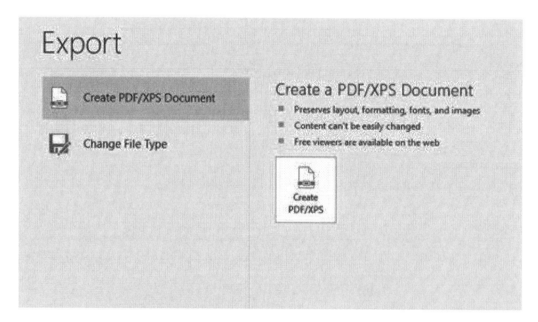

- **Transform:** This allows you to transform your documents into a web page.

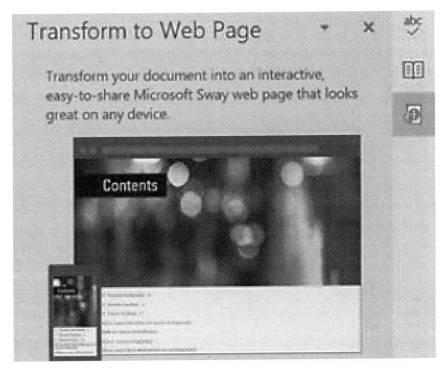

Transform to Web Page

Transform your document into an interactive, easy-to-share Microsoft Sway web page that looks great on any device.

- **Close:** This allows you to close the document you are working on.

Home Tab

File | Home | Insert | Draw | Design | Layout | References | Mailings | Review | View | Developer | Help

The Home tab is the default tab displayed in Word 365. The Home tab contains the following features.

- **Clipboard**: The clipboard ribbon allows you to use the options stated below

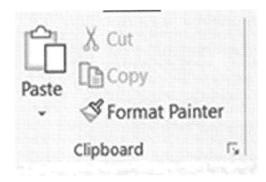

- **Cut**: remove a selected portion of the document and save it into the clipboard.

- **Copy**: To make another document copy and then save it on the clipboard.

- **Format painter**: By doing so, you can convert one text format into another text format.

- **Paste**: This tool Is what produced or displayed the items cut or copied to the right location.

- **Font Ribbon Tab:** The fonts in a Word 365 document can be changed using the tools on the Font ribbon. You can accomplish the following using font ribbon:

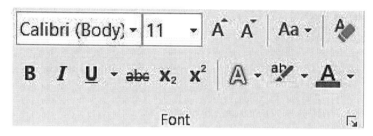

- **Bold:** To make the selected texts bold in the word documents.

- **Italics:** To make selected texts in the word document slant or slope.

- **Underline:** To underline the selected texts in a Word document.

- **Strikethrough:** To cut a line across the selected texts in the Word document

- **Font Style:** You can choose the text style you like using this option.

- **Font Size:** This is used to adjust the font size of a text.

- **Font Color:** This is used to change to font color of your texts.

- **Text Highlighted Color:** This is used to change the background of the selected texts.

- **Subscript:** This is used to type letters or texts below the line.

- **Superscript:** This is used to type letters or texts above the line.

- **Text Effect and Typography:** This option allows you to add some flairs to your texts by applying text effects such as shadow or glow.

- **Change Case:** This is used to change the selected texts to uppercase, lowercase, or other common capitalization.

- **Clear Formatting** eliminates all formatting from the selected texts, leaving the default content in its unformatted state.

- **Paragraph Ribbon Tab:** Using the paragraph editing tools found under the Paragraph tab, you may change the paragraphs in your work by changing things like alignments, bullets, and numbering. listed below

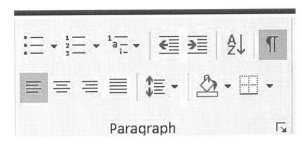

- **Bullet:** The bullet list format from the bullet library is used to build a bullet list.

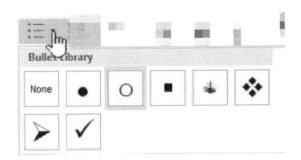

- **Numbering**: Using the numbering list format from the numbering library, this is done to construct a numbering list.

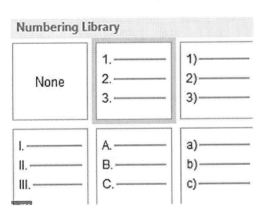

- **Multilevel List**: Using this, you can organize something into a multilayer list or make an outline. This combines both a bulleted and numbered listing.

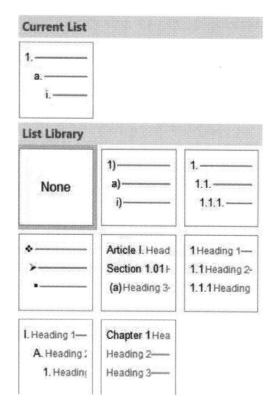

- **Align Left**: This is used to align your texts to the left margin
- **Center**: This is used to place your content at the center
- **Align Right**: This is used to align your texts to the left margin
- **Justify:** To evenly place the content on the left and margin

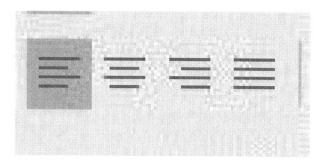

- **Decrease and Increase Indent**: This option allows you to move the paragraph closer or farther away from the margin

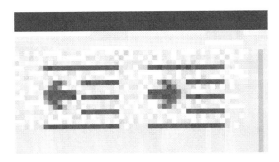

- **Line and Paragraph Spacing:** This is used to set how space appears between lines of texts or between paragraphs

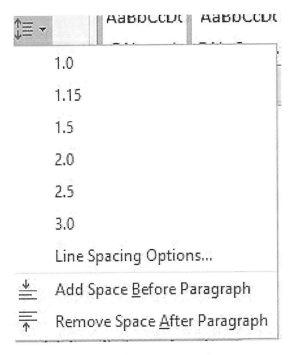

- **Sort:** This arranges the current selection in alphabetical or numerical order.

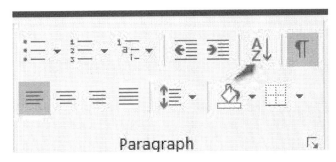

- **Shading:** This is used to change the color behind the selected texts, paragraphs, or tables.

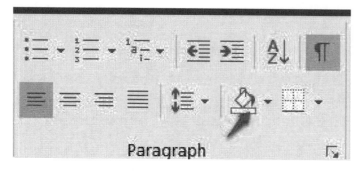

- **Borders**: This option allows you to add or remove borders from your selection. '

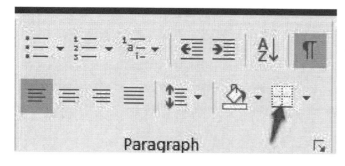

- **Styles:** You can apply this formatting attributes to your tables, texts, and list of documents to alter how they seem.

- **Editing:** The Editing tool allows you to find, replace, and select texts in the documents.

- **Dictate:** This is a new tool in Word 365 that allows you to use speech to type rather than using the keyboard.

Insert Tab

The Insert tab, as the name implies, allows you to insert interesting features to your content on Word 365. The following are the tools in the Insert tab:

- **The Page Ribbon:** The Page ribbon, when clicked on, pops the following;
  - ○ **Cover Page:** This drop-down contains commands such as Built-in, Remove Current Cover Page, and Save Selection to Cover Page Gallery.
  - ○ **Blank Page:** This option allows you to insert two-page breaks into the document; one above the current insertion point and another below.
  - ○ **Page Break:** This allows you to insert the page break instead of displaying the Breaks dialog box.

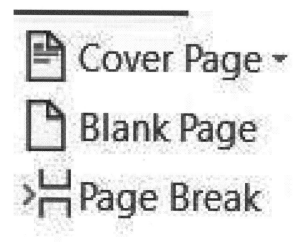

Pages

- **Tables:** This option allows you to insert tables of different sizes and shapes into your content.

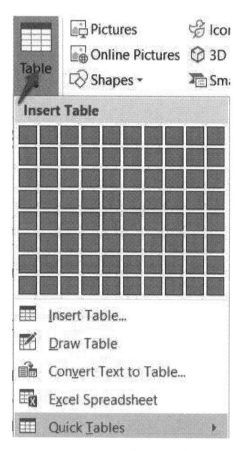

- **Illustration Ribbon:** This option allows you to insert features such as Pictures, Online Pictures, Shapes, Icons, 3D Models, SmartArt, Charts, and screenshots into your documents.

Illustrations

- **Add-ins Ribbon Tab:** With this feature, Microsoft users can merge external application features with Word 365.

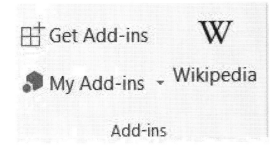

Add-ins

- **Media Ribbon Tab:** This feature can insert online videos into your content.

- **Link Ribbon Tab:** With this feature, you can link creations into other files, webpages, cross-references, etc.

Links

- **Comment Ribbon Tab:** This allows you to add a note about a part of a document.

Comments

- **Header & Footer:** This allows you to insert your document header, footer, and the page number.

Header & Footer

- **Text Ribbon**: This allows you to insert features such as Text Box, Quick Parts, Drop Cap, Signature, etc.

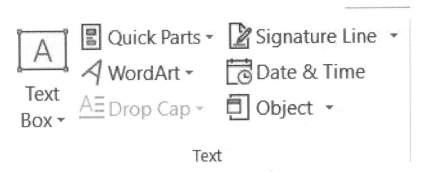

Symbol Ribbon: With this option, you can insert equations and symbols into your documents.

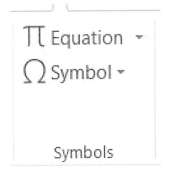

Draw Tab

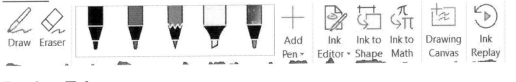 The Draw tab is only available in Word 365. The Draw tab allows you to add notes, create shapes, edit texts, and lots more. The draw tab offers three types of drawing textures; pen, pencil, and highlighter.

Design Tab

The Design tab largely concentrates on adding Quick Styles Texts and Themes to your projects. These are the characteristics of the Design tab.

- **Document Formatting**: When you go to this ribbon, you can use the following features.

- **Themes**: This contains a drop-down list of themes that can be applied to your documents. The drop-down list contains commands such as Built-in, More Themes on Microsoft Office Online, Browse for Themes, and Save Current Themes.

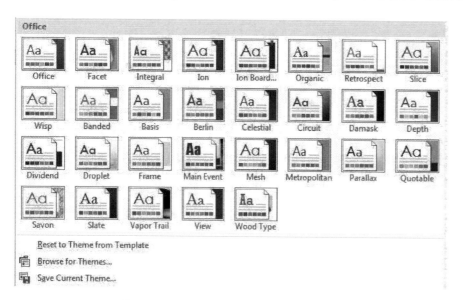

- **Style Set**: This option allows you to change the look of your document by selecting a new style layer. The Style Set affects the font and paragraphs of your document.

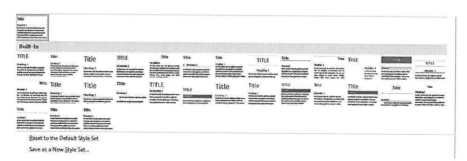

- **Colors**: This option displays the list of all the colors available and allows you to change the color component of the active theme.

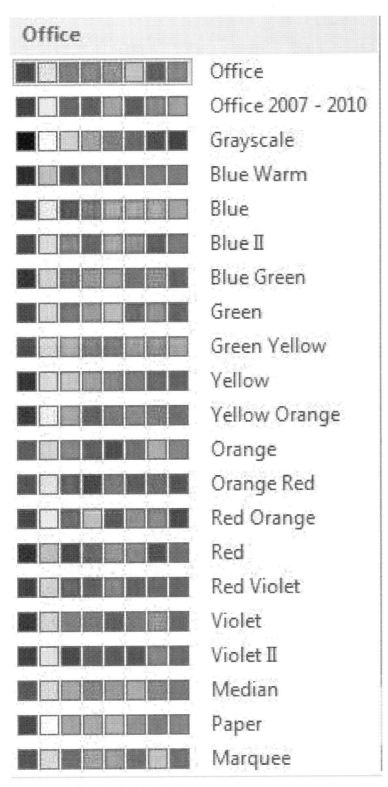

Office

	Office
	Office 2007 - 2010
	Grayscale
	Blue Warm
	Blue
	Blue II
	Blue Green
	Green
	Green Yellow
	Yellow
	Yellow Orange
	Orange
	Orange Red
	Red Orange
	Red
	Red Violet
	Violet
	Violet II
	Median
	Paper
	Marquee

Customize Colors...

- **Font**: This displays a list of all the fonts available and allows you to change the font components of the active theme.

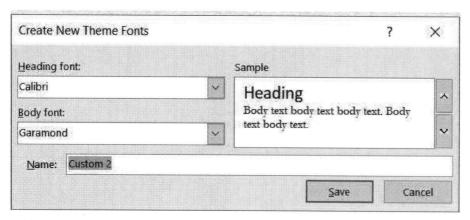

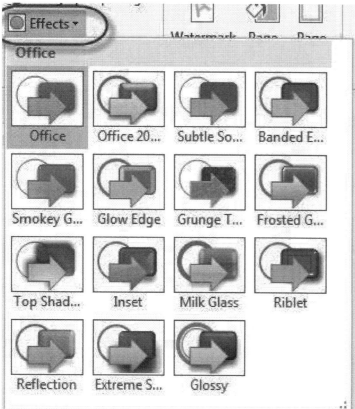

- **Set as Default:** This allows you to use the current look for all the documents.

- **Page Background:** The Page Background ribbon has the following features:

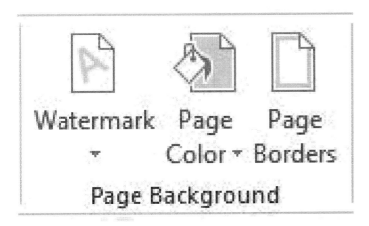

- **Watermark:** This tool adds text or an image to a document's backdrop. The drop-down menu for Watermark offers the following commands: specific watermark. After erasing the watermark, save your selection to the watermark gallery.

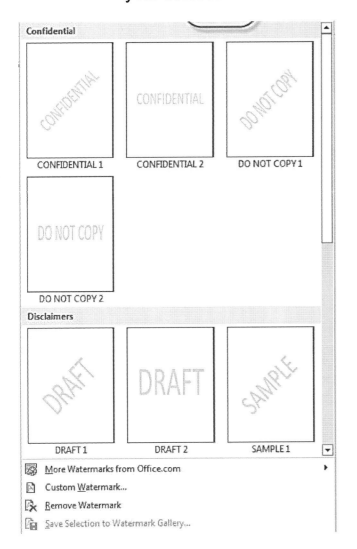

- **Page Color:** This option allows you to change your page's background color and display the full theme color palette.

- **Page Borders:** The Border and Shading dialog box is displayed by this option.

Layout Tab

On the layout tab, there are tools for page configuration, paragraph indent, and spacing adjustments. The subsequent components are located under the layout tab:

- **Page Setup:** Here, the Margin and Page Setup dialog boxes are shown.

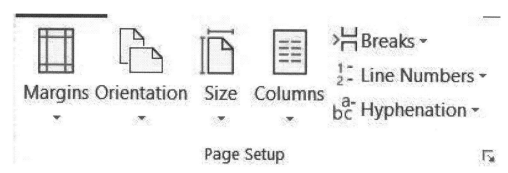

- **Margins:** You can do this by selecting one of the built-in margin settings or customizing your margin.

- **Orientation:** This is where you change the orientation of your current document to either Portrait or landscape.

- **Size:** This is where you select the paper size from the available paper sizes.

- **Columns:** This is where you split your documents into two or more columns.

- **Breaks:** This enables you to choose instructions like "Page Break," "Remove Page Break," and "Reset All Page Breaks" from a drop-down list.

- **Line Numbers:** Here, you can select from the drop-down list commands such as None, Continuous, Restart Each Page, Restart Each Section, etc.

- **Hyphenation:** This option moves your texts to the next line when it exceeds the space. This option contains commands such as None. Automatic, Manual, and Hyphenation Options.

- **Paragraph:** This displays the Paragraph dialog box, Indent, and Spacing tab.

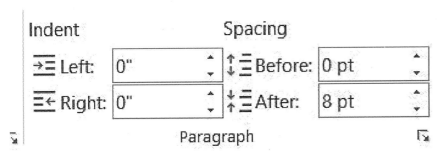

- **Indent**: This option determines how much indentation is to be applied to the paragraph of the current selection in the document, whether to the left or right.

- **Spacing**: This option specifies how much left- or right-spacing should be used for the paragraph of the selected document.

- **Arrange:** The Arrange group contains the following features.

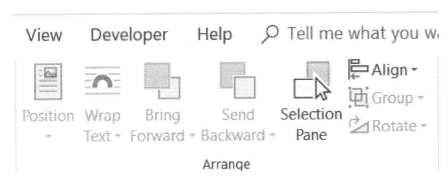

- **Position**: This menu item shows many photo placement options in a document, including Line With Text and Text Wrapping.

- **Wrap Text**: The commands in this option, which control how texts wrap around objects, are as follows: Square, Tight, Through, In Line with Text, etc.

- **Bring Forward**: This option brings the selected object forward one level so that it is hidden behind fewer objects.

- **Send Backward**: By choosing this option, the chosen object is lowered by one level and concealed behind further objects.

- **Selection Pane**: This displays the list of all your objects. This option allows you to select the objects, change the order, and show visibility.

- **Align**: This allows you to change the placements of your selected objects in the documents.

- **Group:** This allows you to join, move, and format objects as if they were a single object.

- **Rotate**: This option allows you to rotate or flip the selected objects.

Reference Tab

The Reference tab allows you to use all the commands for creating references in your documents. The following are the commands available in the Reference tab

- **Table of Contents:** The following features are found in the Table of content group

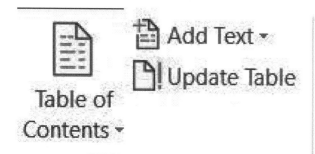

- **Table of Content:** By including a table of contents, this option allows you to get an overview of your paper. Built-in, Insert Table of Content, and Save Selection to Table of Contents Gallery are some options available in the drop-down menu.

- **Add Text:** This helps to add the current heading in the Table of content.

- **Update Table:** You can use this option to update the table of contents so that each entry now refers to the appropriate page number.

- **Footnotes:** You can display the Footnote and Endnote dialog box. The following are the features available in the Footnotes group

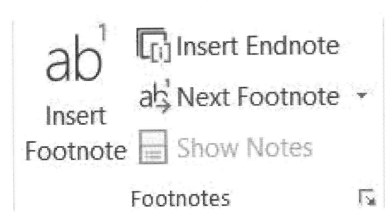

- **Insert Footnote:** This option allows you to provide information about anything in your document by adding a note on the current page of the document.

- **Insert Endnote:** This enables you to include notes after the text to add additional information about something, such as comments and citations.

- **Next Footnote:** You can jump to the next footnote with this option.

- **Show Notes:** This shows where the document's footnotes and endnotes are.

- **Research:** The following are the features of the Research group:

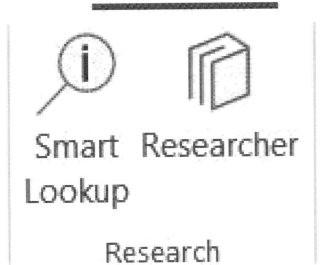

- **Smart Lookup:** This allows you to definitions, images, web pages, and other results from different online sources.

- **Citations and Bibliography:** The following are the features of Citations and Bibliography.

Citations & Bibliography

- **Insert Citation**; This enables you to cite the book, article, or other materials that an information source is based on when referencing.

- **Manage Source**: This organizes the sources cited in your document.

- **Style:** This allows you to choose the style of your citations in the documents.

- **A bibliography** lists your sources in a bibliography or a work cited section.

- **Captions:** The following are the features in the Caption group

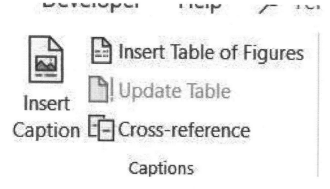

Captions

- **Insert Caption:** This allows you to insert or add a caption below a picture or graphics to give a short description.

- **Insert Table of Figures:** For quick reference, insert a list of captioned objects and their page numbers.

- **Update Table:** To update the table of figures to include all the entries in the documents.

- **Cross-reference:** To refer to specific places in your document, such as headings, figures, and tables.

- **Index:** The following are the features in the Index group

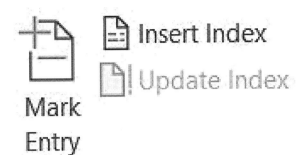

Index

- **Mark Entry:** This is used to mark the selected texts to the index in the documents.

- **Insert Index:** This is used to add or insert index listing keywords and page numbers they appear on.

- **Update Index:** By doing this, the index is updated to reflect the current page number for each entry.

- **Table of Authorities:** The following are the features of the Table of Authorities group:

- **Mark Citation:** This is used to add the selected texts to the Table of Authority.

- **Insert Table of Authorities:** A table of authority for the instances, laws and other sources listed in the papers is added or inserted using this method.

- **Update Table:** This is used to update the table of authorities to add all the citations.

Mailings Tab

This tab is in charge of capping off a successful mail run. The features found in the Mailing tab are listed below.

- **Create:** The Create group is focused on creating envelopes and labels.

Envelopes Labels

Create

- **Envelopes:** This allows you to create and print envelopes in different sizes. You can also format the address and add electronic postage to it.

- **Labels:** This also allows you to create and print labels in different sizes.

- **Start Mail Merge**: Finalizing a successful mail range is the responsibility of this tab. The options available on the Mailing tab are listed below.

Start Mail   Select   Edit
Merge ▾ Recipients ▾ Recipient List

Start Mail Merge

- **Start Mail Merge:** This is used to create a document you intend to send to multiple people. The drop-down contains commands such as Letters, E-mail messages, Envelopes, etc.

- **Select Recipients:** This option allows you to select the list of people you intend to send your documents. You can type a new list, select an existing one, or choose from Outlook contact.

- **Edit Recipient Lists:** This allows you to change your recipient lists or select a certain set of people to get the mails. With this option, you can also sort, filter, find, remove duplicates, and validate addresses on the list.

- **Write & Insert Field:** The Write & Insert Field group commands are only accessible when you are in Mail Merge documents. The following are the features of this group:

- **Highlight Merge Fields:** This is used to highlight the field in your documents. This option allows you to easily identify where contents from your recipient list will be inserted.

- **Address Block:** This allows you to add an address to your letter. You can also indicate the format and location of the list

- **Greeting Line:** This allows you to add a greeting to your documents.

- **Insert Merge Field:** This enables you to include a recipient list field in the papers. These fields include Last Name, Home Phone, and Company Name.

- **Rules:** This allows you to add rules such as Ask, If, Then, etc. to the mail merge.

- **Match Field:** This allows you to match the required field with the recipient list.

- **Update Labels:** This updates all the labels in the document to correspond with the information from the recipient list.

- **Preview Result:** The following are the features of the Preview Results group:

Find Recipient

Check for Errors

Preview Results

- **Preview Results** insert data from your recipient list into the merged field. This option cannot work when there is no field in the documents.

- **First Record**: This is used to view the first record in the recipient list.

- **Previous Record**: This is used to view the previous record in the recipient list.

- **Go to Record**: This is used to view a specific record in the recipient list.

- **Next Record**: This is used to view the next record in the recipient list.

- **Last Record:** This is used to view the last record in the recipient list.

- **Find Recipient:** This is used to find a specific recipient and locate the recipient document to view.

- **Check Errors:** This option tells Word 365 how to deal with errors during mail merge. This also checks for errors in the mail merge.

- **Finish:** This group only has one feature;

Finish

- **Finish & Merge:** This allows you to choose how you want to finalize the mail merge, either by opening the mail in a new window, sending the mail to the printer, or sending it via email.

Review Tab

The Review tab is designed to give detailed information about the documents you are working on. The following are the features in the Review tab.

- **Proofing:** The following tools are used for proofing your documents.

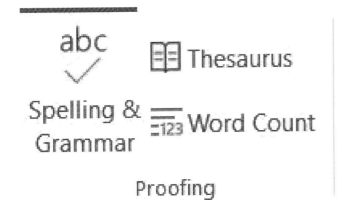

Proofing

- **Spelling & Grammar:** This allows you to check your document's spelling and grammar errors.
- **Thesaurus:** This research service suggests saying what you mean in another way.

- **Word Count:** This counts the document's words, characters, and lines.

- **Accessibility:**
    - **Check Accessibility**: ensure that your file follows accessibility practices.

- **Language:** The following are the features in the Language group

- **Translate:** This helps to translate text into different languages by using bilingual dictionaries and online services.

- **Language:** This helps in choosing the language for proofing tools such as spelling checks.

- **Comments:** The following are the features of the Comments group.

Comments

- **New Comment:** This adds or inserts a note to the active cell selection.

- **Delete:** This is used to delete selected comments in the active selection.

- **Previous:** To move to the previous comment.

- **Next:** To move to the next comment

- **Show Comments:** To view all the comments in the documents.

- **Tracking:** The following are the features of the Tracking group;

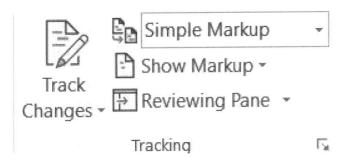

Tracking

- **Track Changes:** This allows you to keep track of changes that occur in the documents.

- **Display for Review:** This contains the drop-down commands on how you like to see changes in your document.

- **Show Markup:** This option allows you to choose the types of markup to display in your documents.

- **Receiving Panel:** This displays all the changes made to your documents in a list.

- **Changes:** The following are the features in the Changes group

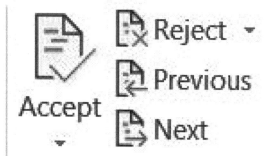

Changes

- **Accept:** This accepts the change tracked and then moves to the next.
- **Reject:** This undoes the change tracked and then moves to the next.
- **Previous:** This moves to the previous tracked change
- **Next:** This moves to the next tracked change

- **Compare:** The Compare group contains the following feature
  - **Compare:** This is used to compare two documents to see their similarities. Also, with this option, you can combine revisions from many authors to form a single document.

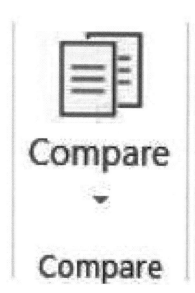

Compare

- **Protect:** The Protect group contains the following features:

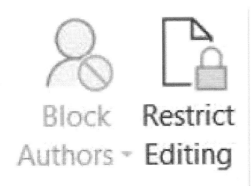

Protect

- **Block Authors:** This option prevents others from making changes to the texts selected in the document

- **Restrict Editing:** This option sets boundaries on how others can make document changes.

- **Resume:** The Resume group has just a feature which is highlighted below

- **Resume Assistant:** This allows the users to get different templates.

View Tab

The View tab contains the feature to preview content, read content, zoom in and out, etc. The following are the features in the View tab.

- **Views:** The Views group contains commands allowing you to view your document differently.

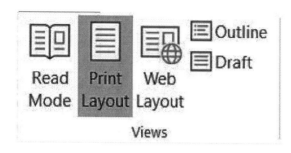

- **Read Mode:** This option is also referred to as Full-Screen Reading. This allows you to maximize the Word window on the screen so that all the toolbars are removed for easy reading of the documents.

- **Print Layout:** This displays the document how it should be when printed out. This is the default view.

- **Web Layout:** This displays how the document should appear on the web page.

- **Outline:** This displays the document in the outline, where content is displayed in a bulleted form.

- **Draft:** This displays the document in draft mode for easy and quick editing. The headers and footers are not visible when the document is displayed in this mode.

- **Immersive:** This Immersive group has just one feature, highlighted below.
    - **Learning Tool:** This tool uses proven techniques to advance reading for people not minding their age and ability.

Learning
Tools

Immersive

- **Show:** The following are the features in the Show group

☐ Ruler

☐ Gridlines

☐ Navigation Pane

Show

- **Ruler:** This is used to display a ruler next to your documents.
- **Gridlines:** This is used to display gridlines in the background of your document for perfect object replacement.
- **Navigation Pane**: This option allows you to move around your document with ease.
- **Zoom:** The Zoom group is concerned about adjusting the display percentage of the active document. The following commands are found in the Zoom group:

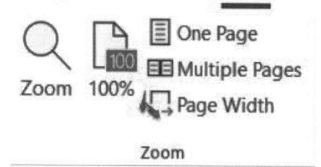

Zoom

- **Zoom:** This tool allows you to zoom your document to the size you want.

- **100%:** This allows you to zoom your document to 100%.

- **One Page:** This allows you to zoom an entire document page to fit in the application window.

- **Two Pages:** This allows you to zoom the two pages of your documents to fit in the application window.

- **Page Width**: This allows you to zoom the width of the page to match the width of the application window.

- **Window:** The Window group contains the following features:

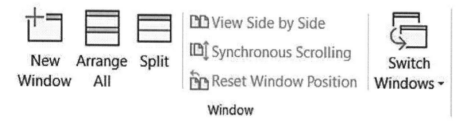

Window

- **New Window:** This allows you to open a new window of the active documents.

- **Arrange All:** This stacks your open windows side by side on the screen so you can see them all at once.

- **Split:** This divides the current window into two parts.

- **View Side by Side:** This allows you to display two documents side by side so they can be easily compared rather than switching back and forth between the documents.

- **Synchronous Scrolling:** This option allows you to compare two documents line by line or scan for differences. Here you get to view two documents side by side.

- **Reset Window Position:** This option allows you to reset the window's position so that the two documents displayed side by side occupy the same level of space.

- **Switch Windows:** This allows you to switch between another open window.

- **Macros:** The Macros group only has one feature, and it is highlighted below
    - **Macros:** This is used to view, record, or pause macro. You can also use this button to view the list of macros

- **SharePoint:** The SharePoint group has one feature, and it is highlighted below:

- **Properties**: This works automatically with contents or documents in SharePoint Online and OneDrive for Business libraries.

Developer Tab

The Developer tab includes additional commands relating to macros and Visual Basic. The following are the features in the Developer tab.

- Code: The following are the features in the Code group

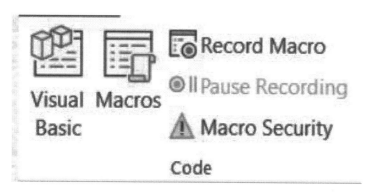

- **Visual Basic**: This is used to open the Visual Basic Editor, which is used to create and edit the VBA macros.

- **Macros**: This shows the list of macros you can work with. Here you can run, edit, and delete macros.

- **Record Macro:** This is used to start or stop recording a macro. This is used to pause the macro recording.

- **Macro Security:** This is used to customize the Macro security settings.

- **Add-ins**: The Add-ins group contains the following features:

Add-ins

- **Add-ins:** This allows you to insert Add-ins and use the web to improve your work.

- **Word Add-Ins:** This option allows you to manage the add-ins available for use with the file.

- **COM Add-Ins:** This allows you to manage the available COM add-ins.

- **Controls:** The following features are found in the Control group:

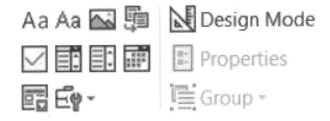

Controls

  ○ **Rich Text**: This button allows you to insert rich text content control.

  ○ **Plain Text**: This button allows you to insert plain content control.

  ○ **Picture**: This button allows you to insert picture content control.

  ○ **Building Block Gallery:** This button allows you to insert building block gallery content control.

- **Check Box:** This button allows you to insert check box content control.

- **Combo Box:** This button allows you to insert combo box content control.

- **Drop Down Box:** This button allows you to insert drop-down box content control.

- **Date Picker:** This button allows you to insert date content control.

- **Repeating Section:** This button allows you to insert content control that contains other controls and repeats the content of the controls as needed.

- **Legacy Tool:** This button allows you to insert ActiveX control or form control.

- **Design Mode:** This allows you to turn off or on the design mode.

- **Control Properties:** This allows you to view or modify the properties of the selected control.

- **Group:** This allows you to group or ungroup a selected text.

- **Mapping:** The Mapping group has one feature, and it is highlighted below:

- **XML Mapping Pane:** This is where the XML data is stored and create content controls that are linked to it in the document.

- **Protect:** The Protect group contains the following features:

- **Block Authors:** This option prevents others from making changes to the texts selected in the document

- **Restrict Editing:** This option sets boundaries on how others can make document changes.

- **Template:** The Template group has just a feature which is highlighted below

- **Document Template:** This allows users to view and change the attached document templates and manage the global template and ads-ins.

Help Tab

47

The Help tab is a newly added Word 365 that offers a solution, contact support, and feedback to Microsoft users. This tab provides fast access to the Help Task Pane and some useful website links.

- **Help & Support:** The following are the features in the Help & Support group:

- **Help:** This allows you to display the Help task pane showing the home page. You can also display this option by pressing F1.

- **Contact Support:** This allows you to display the Help task pane asking for help.

- **Feedback:** This displays the Feedback tab from the File tab.

- **Showing Training:** This displays the Help task pane showing the training videos.

What's New: This shows the most recently installed updates. You can also access this from the File tab and Account.

Book 2: - Excel

Microsoft Office includes the Excel program, which is widely used. It is generally applicable because it is a spreadsheet. It is possible to organize, calculate, and save several data types for later use. You may organize almost any form of data using the Excel grid interface. Excel's power is in its ability to provide complete freedom in designing the layout and structure of the data you wish to organize. The spreadsheet with the highest usage rate worldwide is Microsoft Excel.

With the help of a wide range of arithmetic operations and functions, Excel spreadsheets let you deal with tables of numerical data arranged in columns and rows. You can create pivot tables and macros, use graphing tools, perform basic calculations, and do many more helpful things with Excel. They can also display data graphs, including line graphs, histograms, and bar charts. Mac, Android, Windows, and iOS are just a few operating systems with which Microsoft Excel is compatible.

Data organization and manipulation are made simpler by Microsoft Excel's usage of rows and columns. Spreadsheet rows are represented by numbers, whereas alphabets denote column headings. You can program Excel using Visual Basic for Applications (VBA), and you can retrieve data from other sources using DDE (Microsoft's Dynamic Data Exchange).

Why Use and Learn Excel?

MS Excel is commonly used for various jobs since it is simple to use and allows for the easy addition and removal of information. Excel is a need for anything involving financial activity. Excel is appealing to many individuals because it can be used to create new spreadsheets with customized equations for everything from a straightforward quarterly forecast to a comprehensive corporate annual report. Common information like sales leads, project progress *reports, contact lists, and billing are frequently organized and tracked using Excel.

Finally, using large datasets in science and statistics requires using Excel. Researchers can more quickly do variance analysis and display massive volumes of data by using statistical formulas and graphing tools in Excel. There are countless areas where Microsoft Excel is essential. The following departments demonstrate how important Microsoft Excel is:

Calculations:

When it comes to conducting computations, Microsoft Excel becomes useful. The software includes basic math, statistics, and even engineering tasks. Excel can handle calculations that take multiple iterations to arrive at a final solution by inserting only a few simple formula components.

Create Graphs/Charts:

Different departments can visually portray statistical data using various Microsoft Excel charts.

Formatting:

Excel also includes a tool for formatting cells. The cell formatting function comes in helpful when trying to figure out how things work. If a certain result is found, the cells can be structured to show that way. These are some uses that have been described above.

Microsoft Excel can conduct a wide range of functions and tasks. To this day, spreadsheets are the most effective tools for analyzing data. It's not the sole tool for handling all data tasks, but it's one of the most cost-effective and dependable options available for data analysis. Because it's built on your knowledge of the analytics process, it is a solid basis for generating intelligent data. For this reason, organizations continue to emphasize the significance of Excel as the most intelligent approach to obtaining useful insights. Despite this, the method continues to be beneficial.

Examples of Using Excel

The Microsoft Excel program offers a broad range of functions and capabilities for regular official tasks. Let's look at how different sorts of consumers throughout the globe utilize Microsoft Excel capabilities in their everyday lives.

- **In Education Sector**

Teachers may use table designs, forms, charts, data tools, and algorithms to train students in the classroom. Excel enables pupils to comprehend and resolve basic, logical, mathematical, and statistical problems. Teachers can design a table on an Excel sheet to use as a teaching tool. They might accent important numbers, highlight beautiful cells with color, and display data using bars and charts.

- ## In Business Sector

Does anyone think a business owner can operate their company successfully without using Microsoft Excel, big or small? There are several corporate settings where the Microsoft Excel application is used. Examples of commercial tasks include goal-setting, budgeting, and planning, team management, account management, calculating revenue and expenses, valuing product offerings, and managing client data. In the workplace, Microsoft Excel improves routine administrative procedures' effectiveness, accuracy, and predictability. Excel offers useful features: filters, charts, conditional formatting, pivot tables, and mathematical and financial formulas.

- ## Data Analysis

Data analysis is a major part of working for an online business or website owner (e-commerce, blog, forums, etc.). Tracking website traffic, sales figures, customer feedback, marketing tactics, user activity, and events are just a few examples. It takes a lot of time and thinking to complete a task, especially when things don't go according to plan.

The Microsoft Excel program provides many benefits for users and owners of internet businesses. You can use Excel to aid you with normal daily tasks, including filtering users' data by country, age-selecting customers, applying conditional formulae to large amounts of data, and more.

- ## Goals Setting and Planning

Microsoft Excel allows you to plan goals for your financial, career, and physical well-being. These provide you a distinct focus on which to focus while guiding you in the right direction. Excel spreadsheets, plan documents, and logs are created to complete these actions and tasks and measure progress toward the goal.

MS Excel Interface

The ribbon, which appears as a strip of controls running across the top of the application window, is the focus of the Excel interface. The ribbon is separated into tabs, each with a set of controls to make it easier to find tools. The location of the different tools is designated using this terminology. For example, the Home page, Font grouping, and Bold button may apply a bold font to a text selection. With the Main screen chosen and a workbook open with one blank worksheet, the Microsoft Excel 2022 dialogue box looks like this:

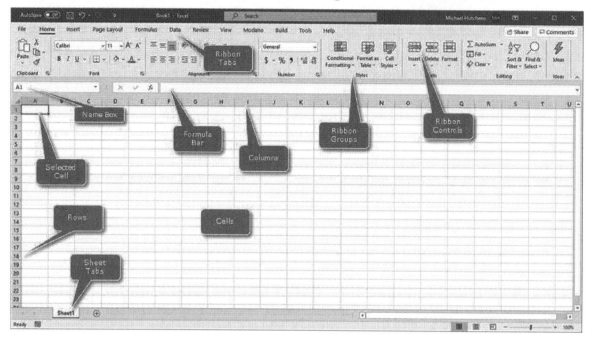

Getting to Know Excel's User Interface

In this part, we'll largely talk about Excel's interface.

The Concept of File Formats

An Excel workbook may be saved in different formats, each with its file extension as discussed in the previous chapters, such as.xlsx or. xlsm.

Click the File tab in the top left corner of the screen, then choose the template sites from the Save As an option to create a new workbook in a specific format or convert an existing workbook to numerous formats. If you prefer, you can open the Save As dialogue box by pressing Alt+F+A and selecting the appropriate file format from the 'Save As' drop-down box.

Contrasting and comparing different file formats

Each Excel file format has a different level of capacity and compatibility with different versions of Excel, which is reflected in its name. It's crucial to keep this in mind while choosing a file format. You should be aware that unless you indicate otherwise when you save a macro-enabled file as an.xlsx file, all the macros in the original file will be erased from the new file.

The following picture compares and contrasts the most commonly used Excel file formats:

File Format	Extension	Compatibility	Functionality
Excel Workbook	.xlsx	Excel 2007 +	Standard file format with macros disabled.
Excel Macro-Enabled workbook	.xlsm	Excel 2007 +	Standard file format with macros enabled.
Excel Binary Workbook	.xlsb	Excel 2007 +	Compressed file format with macros enabled.
Excel 97-2003 Workbook	.xls	Excel 97 +	Standard Excel 97 -2003 file format with macros enabled.
CSV (Comma delimited)	.csv	Excel 97 +	Stores tabular data in plain-text form, separated by a comma.

Changing the Cell's Content

Each cell in a worksheet may contain a constant. However, instead of "hard-codes" or "inputs," the term "constants" should be used since it is the most accurate and least confusing. The following section shows examples of constant and formula cell contents, with the formula bar displaying the contents of each cell.

Cell content may always be added and changed in the toolbar by typing or changing the text in the formula bar and pressing Enter after each insertion or change. In some quarters, this is regarded as "entering" data, whereas "inputting" is the more appropriate and less confusing term.

If you look at the formula in cell A3, you may refer to cell A2 by typing '=' and then typing 'A2' or clicking on cell A2 with the mouse.

The sample on the right also demonstrates Formula Edit Mode. As you can see for cell A2 in this example, Excel enters Formula Edit Mode during the data input process, which makes it simpler to develop formulae by momentarily covering prior ranges with colored boxes while the data is inputted. Select the cell you want to modify, then type or click the F2 key to bring up the Formula Editor box to enter Formula, Modify Mode.

Parts of the Screen Identification

The methods for identifying screen sections are as follows:

Toolbar with quick access buttons

The Quick Access Toolbar (QAT) default has buttons for saving, undoing, and redoing actions. However, you may tailor the toolbar to your requirements by clicking the buttons at the end of the bar and adding your buttons or by right-clicking an icon on any tab and choosing Add to Quick Access toolbar from the context menu that appears. To eliminate a button from your QAT toolbar, right-click on it and choose Delete from the Quick Access toolbar from the context menu that appears.

Tabs

Command keys are arranged into tabs for convenience. For example, those commands used for storing, printing, and transferring files are all found under the File tab. The most often used command options for altering and editing your worksheet are those found on the Home tab.

Ribbon

Every one of the command keys is included inside the Ribbon, which is located on each tab. It is possible that you will not require all of the instructions on a Ribbon. You will begin to recognize that you are simply using what you need. In addition, if you choose, you may also include them in the QAT toolbar.

Table headers, row numbers, and cell addresses.

Each column is identified by a phonetic alphabet, represented by the header bar. The Row number bar is located on the left-hand side of the screen, and it is used to identify each row with a unique number. A cell is a point at which a column and a row cross. For example, the first cell in row 1 of column A is called cell A1. Cell B3 is located on the third row of column B. And so on.

Cell Selection

The cell selection is a heavily outlined rectangle representing the document's current working place. Using the left mouse button to select a cell and the arrow keys to move the cell pointer are acceptable methods of repositioning it. By dragging the mouse cursor over the selection, the cell pointer may be expanded to encompass several cells. If you look closely, you'll see that the row number & column letter "glow up" show where the cell pointer is now.

Formula bar

It is a tool that allows you to enter formulas into a program. The contents of the chosen cell are shown in the formula bar. If a calculation is included inside a cell, the formula bar will display the formula, while the particular cell in the grid region will display the result. To make changes to the contents of a cell, you may click inside the formula bar.

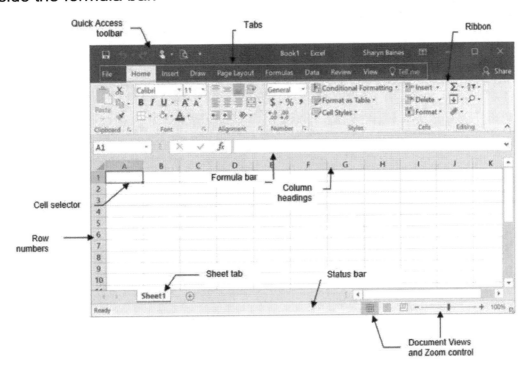

Sheet Tabs

Sheet tabs (worksheets) are used to organize and analyze data in a spreadsheet. For example, it is possible to create unique spreadsheets for each week of the year or for each employee. When you develop a new worksheet (file) in Excel 2022, you will only be provided one worksheet to work with. Selecting the Insert worksheet option, you may quickly and conveniently add to your existing worksheets.

The status bars

It displays current information. The information is shown in the Status bar changes based on what you are doing in the spreadsheet at the time. Example: If you have chosen several cells with values, the Status bar will display the total, average, and number of cells that have been selected in that row. In my essay Find the Average, Count, and Total of a Range without Writing a Formula, I go into further detail on how to do this task.

Viewing the document and controlling the zoom level

To modify the layout or magnification of your screen, use the Documents view buttons and the Zoom control settings on your keyboard. If you are messing with the view buttons, remember to always return to the Normal view to come back to Excel's default view when you are finished. Check out our entries on How to input information into an Excel worksheet. Select cells and navigate around an Excel worksheet if you want to learn more about using spreadsheet programs.

Header Bar / Title Bar

In a graphical user interface, the title bar is a horizontal bar that displays at the top of the screen (GUI). It displays the program's title, the name of the currently open document, or other data that identifies the contents of the window in which it is shown.

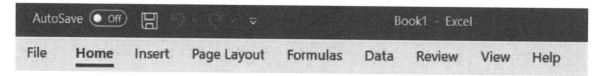

The title bar in the screenshot below displays the software name "TextPad" and the currently edited file name "Document1," but the remainder of the window is blank.

Tabs for Worksheets

When we open an excel workbook, we see a row of rectangular tabs representing a separate worksheet that may be changed. By default, the worksheet will have three spreadsheet tabs open, but we may add more by clicking the add button at the end of each tab and renaming or removing any spreadsheet tabs we've created.

The Excel application is built based on worksheets. These worksheets have their tabs; every excel file must have at least one worksheet to operate correctly. The worksheet tab in Excel may also be used for various purposes, which may be found at the bottom of every Excel spreadsheet tab.

Ribbon Tabs

A ribbon is a group of Excel features related to a particular ribbon tab. The Home ribbon is separated into categories such as Clipboard, Alignment, Font, Number, and so on, as shown in Figure 1. One or more icons in each category correlate to Excel features. For example, click on a cell in a worksheet, then on the center icon in the Alignment group on the Home ribbon to center the content of that cell. This series of actions is abbreviated as Home > Alignment Center.

Similarly, you may merge two adjoining cells by choosing Home > Alignment > Merge & Center and highlighting the two cells; the two cells are then united, and items put in the merged cell are centered. Home > Cells may also insert, format, and remove cells, columns, rows, and worksheets.

There are shortcuts for certain icons. To center the contents of a cell, for example, click on the cell and then press Ctrl-E. To figure out what an icon is for, hover the mouse cursor over it (without clicking). A tooltip with information about the icon will appear.

On a ribbon, a little arrow appears adjacent to some of the clusters (to the right of the group's name). When you click this arrow, a dialogue box will appear with numerous options for you to choose from. Selecting the arrow for the Font group on the Home ribbon, for example, produces a dialogue box with tabs titled Number, Font, Alignment, Border, and so on.

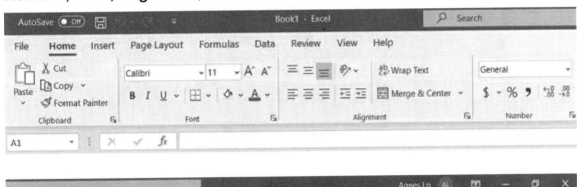

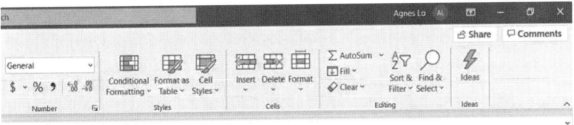

File, Insert, Home, Page Layout, Data, Formulas, Review, View, and Help are the nine tabs on the Excel Ribbon. The Home tab is the default tab when Excel is initially opened.

• **File** - The backstage view of this program allows you to create a new spreadsheet, open a document, save the document, print the document, and export a file.

• **Home** - The most significant or frequently used Excel commands, such as structure, font kinds, and filtering, are all included in this section. The Clipboard group, for example, has commands to cut, copy, and paste, while the Font group contains commands to modify font style, color, and size. Similar functions are grouped. Please bear in mind that depending on the size of your screen and the size of your Excel session (when you lower the size of your Spreadsheet window, fewer buttons appear), your ribbon options may appear differently.

• **Insert -** Users may use this tool to add Pivot Tables, pictures, and shapes to a spreadsheet, as well as charts, graphs, and symbols.

• **Page Layout -** Users may change the margins, color themes, gridlines, and printing area, among other things, to customize the spreadsheet look. When the document is printed, the changes are also applicable.

• **Formulas -** The function library, which also contains some control settings, organizes all key formulas into categories and makes them accessible through the function library.

• **Data -** This function allows users to manage data inside the current spreadsheet and import data from other sources into the file.

• **Review -** Users may use this to do a range of control functions, including spell checking, translation, adding comments and notes, recording changes, and activating worksheet protection, to name a few.

• **View -** Gridlines, zooming, freezing panes, and moving between windows are just a few options for viewing the spreadsheets.

• **Help -** This allows you to access Microsoft's technical support. It allows you to provide feedback for the community and suggest a feature.

About Spreadsheets

A spreadsheet in Microsoft Excel is just a worksheet divided into numerous rows and columns to record data about a company's inventory, income and expenditures, debts, and credit card balances, among other things. Electronic spreadsheets have mostly replaced outmoded paper-based worksheets in today's business world.

A Microsoft Excel spreadsheet comprises three parts: rows, columns, and cells, which are the intersections of these columns and rows. To identify them from one another, column labels are usually letters (A, B, C, D,) while row labels are numbers (1, 2, 3, 4). A cell is generated by the intersection of two columns and two rows in an MS Excel spreadsheet.

A cell is the intersection of two columns and two rows in an MS Spreadsheet. Every cell has been given an address that contains the cell's column name and row number. Keep in mind that in a cell's address, the column letter will come first, and the row number will come second. An Excel 2022 file has almost 18 billion cells, making it the world's biggest spreadsheet.

About Cells

A cell, in general, is a rectangular area formed by the intersection of two columns and two rows. The Cell Name (or Reference, which may be formed by combining the Column Letter solely with the Row Number) and the Row Number are two identifiers for cells. For example, the cell in Column "C" in Row 3 would be identified as cell C3. A cell may include labels, numbers, formulae, and functions.

Name of the Cell - The cell reference is set to the name of the cell by default. You may, however, give an individual cell or set of cells in your spreadsheet a different name. The alternate name may then be used in formulas and functions to provide a quick way to get to a specific part of the spreadsheet.

Reference for Cells - By combining the Column Letter and the Row Number into a single string of letters, you may get the cell's identity. For example, the cell in Column "C" in Row 3 would be identified as cell C3.

Rows and Columns

A row is a horizontal line that runs across the page in the grid design of a worksheet in MS Excel. Numeric numerals, such as 1, 2, and 3, are used to distinguish them on the horizontal rows. To identify them from one another, vertical columns are labeled with alphabetical values such as A, B, and C.

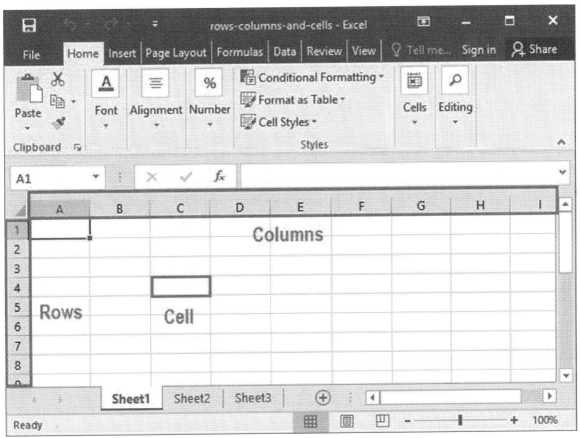

Each row in the worksheet has its row number, which may be used as a component of a cell reference, such as A2, A1, or M16. You may choose a whole row of data by touching the row header. We picked row number three in the preceding example. Inserting, deleting, covering, unhiding, and resizing rows, as well as filters and conditional formatting, are just a few of the things you can do with rows in Excel. This page lists topics that will show you how to use rows in Microsoft Office Excel.

The Second important thing about cell location is getting to know Column and how to read it. Each column on the worksheet, located at the top of the page, is represented and identified by recognizable alphabetical header letters. The columns on the spreadsheet screen are arranged vertically. An Excel spreadsheet has 256 columns, each labeled with a letter from the alphabet. The column labels lead to the letters "AA," "AC," "AB," "AD," and "BC," "BA," "BB," "BD," and so on until they reach the letter "Z." As a result, the column headers are designated A through XFD. The spreadsheet's columns are aligned vertically, showing data from top to bottom.

Book 3: - PowerPoint

When starting any activity in PowerPoint, you must launch the program either from scratch, also known as a blank document or from a preset template that, depending on the type of template you choose, comes with a specified model

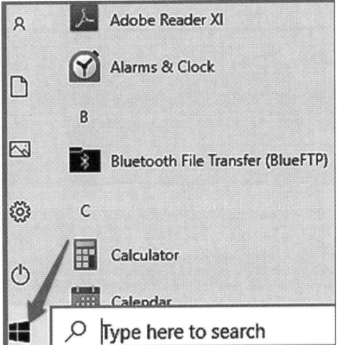

and layout.

    a. To start any activity on PowerPoint, you must launch the program and choose between starting from scratch, often known as a blank project, or selecting a preset template with a specified model and formatting based on the template you choose.

Search for the PowerPoint icon in the available programs by going to the application list and scrolling through it.

    b. Click on the **PowerPoint** icon to launch the application

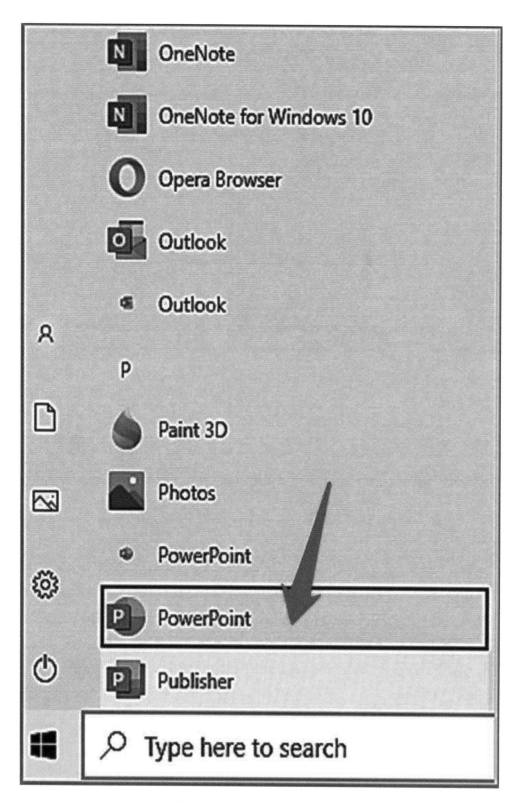

d. You will see the PowerPoint launching screen as soon as you click on the Microsoft icon for PowerPoint. Tap on Blank Presentation to start a new presentation and start organizing it.

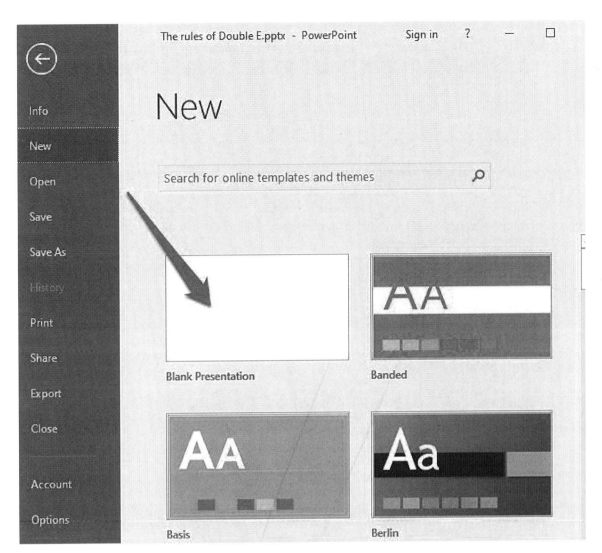

e. The result of the above is the **new blank presentation document** on the main screen, as shown below.

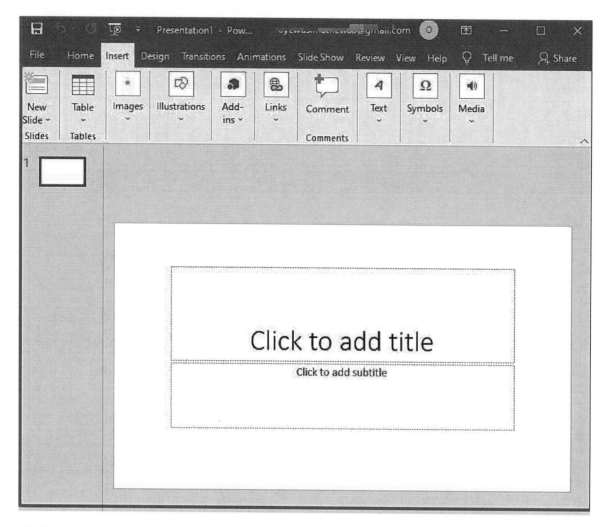

CREATING POWERPOINT FROM THE PRESET TEMPLATE

To create PowerPoint with a preset template that has a specific PowerPoint model and formatting, simply:

a. Click on **any available template** of your choice from the "**start or Open screen**".

b. You can also search for more templates by using the **search box** on the **start screen**.

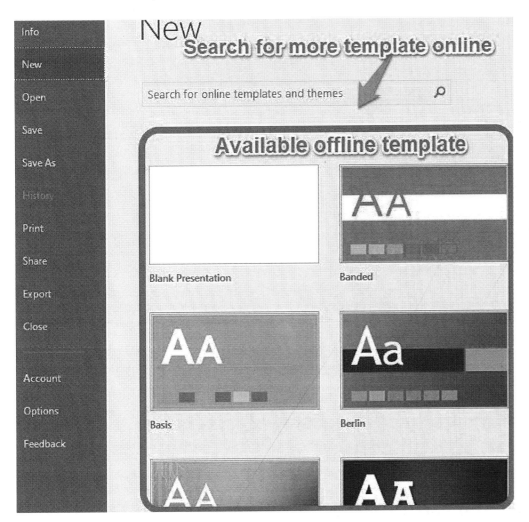

c. As soon as you click on a particular template, you will be shifted to the next screen, as shown below.

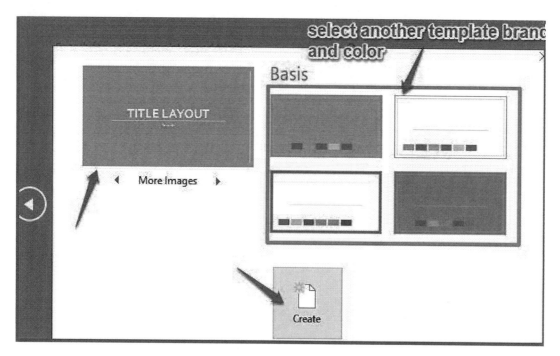

d. If you are okay with that color, tap on **create**, but if not, you can click on other **brands of color**, then tap on **Create**.

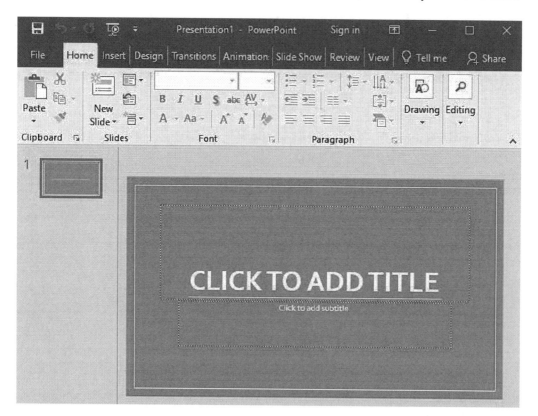

Note: You can create a personal template for yourself and save it. It will also be displayed on the start screen under the personal tab. The personal tab will not appear on the main screen until you create at least a single template.

STUDYING POWERPOINT USER INTERFACE

Immediately you press Esc or Blank presentation from the start screen, you will be taken to the main screen, also known as User Interface, where all PowerPoint works will be executed.

1. **The Title bar:** By default, it will display information about the title of the PowerPoint presentation you are working with in the form of presentations 1, 2, 3, and so on. However, as soon as you save it with a name, the default name will change to the new name you save it with.

2. **Quick Access Toolbar (QAT):** This toolbar enables you to quickly access a certain command that you frequently use whenever the need arises. Some actions, such as redo, open, save, and others, are already in QAT by default.

3. **Ribbon:** it contains the major command of PowerPoint applications that are grouped into tabs according to a particular function that each tab is designed for. Each tab also has various sub-grouping under them. That sub-grouping will appear as you click on the main tab, such as the **Home tab, File and backstage tab, Animation tab, and others.**

4. **File menu and backstage tab:** this is one of the Ribbon tabs, but it is a special tab because it will switch the main screen view to a **backstage view** as soon as you click on it, as it is seen below, and it contains various commands such as **Save, Open, print, Option and many more.**

5. **Slide Area:** this is the main working area. It is divided into the **title and subtitle placeholder, the area showing** the active slide.

6. **Slide pane:** it displays **thumbnails** of all slides in the active or open slide presentation.

Note: if your slide pane is hidden, click on the **View tab** and select the **Normal view button** to make it visible.

7. **Task pane** usually comes up when you select some specific sub-ribbon tab, showing the tools for the sub-ribbon selected. For instance, if you click on the **animation pane** from the **Animation tab**, the task pane will show the available tools under the animation pane, as seen below.

8. **Note Pane:** it is situated at the bottom-right of the active slide with the inscription **"Click to Add Note "**. It is used to add some notes

to the current slide, they are not visible during the slide show, but they are visible when you switch to the **normal view and notes page.**

9. **The Status bar:** the status bar is located below the PowerPoint presentation window. It provides information about the open presentation, such as **slide number** and the **slide's theme.** It also contains Zoom and Views options such as Normal view, Reading view, Slide show, and Slider sorter. I will attend to the View and Zoom options in detail as we move further.

10. **Mini toolbar:** this toolbar is hidden by default but will come up and be visible when you right-click on **selected texts** or when you hover over the **selected text**.

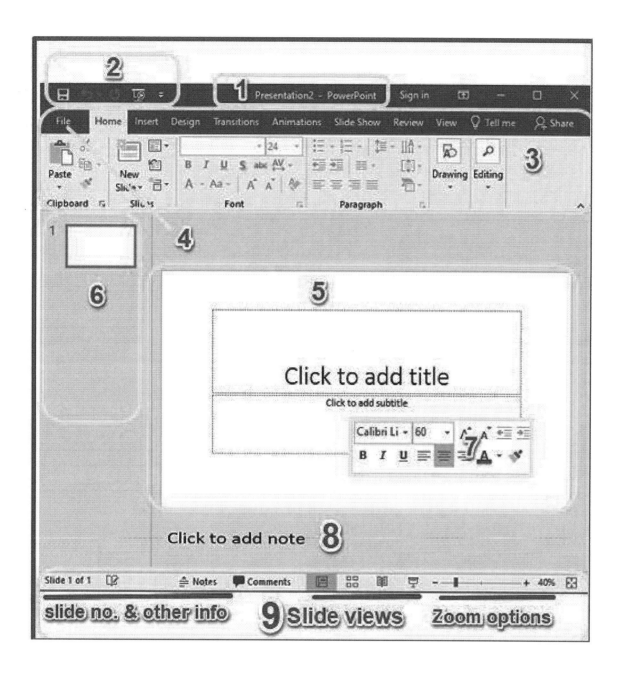

Keyboard Shortcut Commands

Working with Keyboard shortcut commands can reduce your stress, save your time and increase your productivity to a huge extent. Below are the top shortcut commands you can use to work smartly in PowerPoint.

SN	Shortcut Keys	Functions
1.	**Ctrl + A**	To select all the contents of a slide or text placeholder
2.	**Ctrl + B**	To bold the highlighted texts
3.	**Ctrl + C**	To copy the selected item
4.	**Ctrl + D**	To duplicate the active slide
5.	**Ctrl + E**	To center align the selected text
6.	**Ctrl + F**	To open the **Find** dialog box
	Ctrl + G	To group selected items

7.		
8.	**Ctrl + H**	To open the **Replace** dialog box.
9.	**Ctrl + I**	To italicize highlighted text
10.	**Ctrl + J**	To justify aligning selected content
11.	**Ctrl + K**	To open the **Insert Hyperlink** dialog box.
12.	**Ctrl + L**	To left-align selected text.
13.	**Ctrl + M**	To insert a new blank slide
14.	**Ctrl + N**	To create a new blank presentation
15.	**Ctrl + O**	To open an existing presentation
16.	**Ctrl + P**	To go to **the Print** tab in the backstage view
17.	**Ctrl + Q**	To close the presentation
18.	**Ctrl + R**	To the right, align selected text
19.	**Ctrl + S**	To save your presentation
20.	**Ctrl + T**	To open the Font dialog box
21.	**Ctrl + U**	To underline the selected text.
22.	**Ctrl + V**	To paste what you copied last.
23.	**Ctrl + W**	To close your presentation
24.	**Ctrl + X**	To cut selected item

25.	**Ctrl + Y**	To redo the last action, you undo it.
26.	**Ctrl + Z**	To undo your last action
27.	**Ctrl + Shift +C**	To copy Format
28.	**Ctrl + Shift + G**	To Ungroup Selected items
29.	**Ctrl + Shift + F**	To open the Fonts tab of the **Format Cells** dialog box.
30.	**Ctrl + Shift + >**	To increase the selected text font size
31.	**Ctrl + Shift + <**	To decrease the selected text font size
32.	**PgDn**	To move to the next slide
33.	**PgUp**	To go to the Previous Page
34.	**Shift + F3**	To toggle the selected test cases
35.	**Shift F10**	To display the context menu
36.	**Esc**	To cancel an active command
37.	**F1**	To open Microsoft PowerPoint **Help**
38.	**F5**	To go to the slideshow view of the presentation
39.	**F7**	To open the Spelling checker pane
40.	**Alt + F4**	To Exit your presentation

41.	**Alt + W + Q**	To open the Zoom dialog box.
42.	**Alt + Shift + V**	To paste formatting only to another Shape
43.	**Alt + Ctrl + Shift + >**	Superscript selected item
44.	**Alt + Ctrl + Shift + <**	Subscript selected item
45.	**Alt + F**	To go to the **File** tab
46.	**Alt + H**	To go to the **Home** tab
47.	**Alt + N**	To go to the **Insert** tab
48.	**Alt + G**	To go to the **Design** tab
49.	**Alt + T**	To go to the **Transition** tab
50.	**Alt + A**	To go to the **Animation** tab
51.	**Alt + S**	To go to the **Slideshow** tab
52.	**Alt + R**	To go to the **Review** tab
53.	**Alt+ W**	To go to the **View** tab
54.	**Alt + Q**	To search item

Book 4: - OneNote

Microsoft OneNote, a new addition to the Office software family, appears to be nothing more than a digital journal where you may scribble notes and make doodles. That isn't exactly true. OneNote can be utilized similarly to a yellow legal pad. Take notes, make drawings, underline stuff, and scratch it out. But OneNote is so much more.

You can use OneNote to highlight important information in your notes so you can later find it by searching for it. You can add photographs, move notes between sections and pages, copy and paste information from Internet Explorer, and even create tasks in Outlook from your notes. All of these elements will be briefly discussed in this section.

This section will cover the OneNote interface and toolbars. You'll discover how to make a notebook with numerous parts and pages quickly and easily, as well as how to add notes (written or typed), customize your notebooks, and more.

We'll learn about OneNote's advantages and the various versions and platforms on which we can use it. For you to know what's available, we'll become familiar with all of OneNote's menus and functions.

Next, we'll learn how to structure our notebooks so that they have the right amount of sections and pages and how to add content to the pages of our notebooks using a variety of techniques. We'll also discover how to use OneNote's handwriting feature and personalize how our pages and content look.

What exactly is OneNote?

OneNote is a special Microsoft product. But first, let's look at why OneNote is valuable before you can get a feel for it.

We are inundated with an enormous amount of information in numerous daily formats. The overabundance of information has various practical ramifications, including: Where do we keep track of this data? How can we stay on top of what's important to us? In this chapter, I'll show why taking notes is often a good solution to these issues.

Microsoft OneNote is a fantastic tool for keeping track of information in one place while taking notes. Here are some examples of how it has been used:

Projects and meetings: You can keep track of everything you need to finish a project in OneNote. Meeting minutes and communications can be stored with diagrams or photos, document attachments, and links to pertinent files or websites; most of all, this material can be shared with everyone working on the project.

Ideas: Record them in OneNote as you have them. Organize these concepts so that they are all in one location and easy to access, making it easier for you to start working on them.

When visiting the doctor, record any pertinent medical information for you or your family by taking pictures of prescriptions or making notes. You can include links to online research in these comments as well. Recipes are yet another excellent example of how to use a OneNote notebook. Using the built-in camera to take a picture of an existing recipe card or page in a book, you may rapidly capture recipes. Additionally, you can record a conversation about ingredients or recipe ideas or link to a webpage with your preferred dish.

Why should you use OneNote as a digital notebook?

Given that OneNote is free, anyone can use it. This software is bundled with Microsoft 365 and Windows 10, but you may also get it for nothing from Microsoft's website. Whether we use OneNote to keep notes for ourselves or to share with others, it is a fantastic tool that is a core part of Microsoft 365 and seamlessly integrates with Microsoft Teams and Outlook. To keep track of all changes and references on a collaborative project, use OneNote rather than Outlook to distribute project information. This example demonstrates OneNote's ability to produce top-notch solutions.

We maintain track of our notes using pen and paper, note-taking apps on our phones (like Apple Notes), and rival apps like Evernote in addition to OneNote. The drawback of using these other note-taking programs is that they might not be readily available when needed and could not be as closely related to your current task as OneNote is.

The Benefits of Using OneNote

Searchability: We may easily search for a word, phrase, or even a specific tag like essential or inquiry in OneNote. My mantra for the program is "find anything quickly." In this circumstance, marking numerous notes as inquiries or essentials enables you to find those marked notes in the future easily.

Evernote's search function and OneNote's search tool are extremely comparable in searching for words, phrases, or tags, highlighting the obvious benefits of using digital notetaking tools like these. The searchability of pen-and-paper note-taking is one of its main shortcomings, making it difficult and time-consuming to browse through old notes. Additionally, even though the Apple Notes app allows you to search for words, you cannot search for critical notes or any other type of note.

Organization: OneNote's main focus is organization. To make your notes more visible and accessible, you can arrange them differently. Not only can you search for notes by title or page name, but you can also organize similar note pages together using sections. Additionally, you have the search tool, which, as already mentioned, can help you find almost anything.

Contrarily, most other note-taking programs don't offer organizational options; thus, you'll need to give your note's title as much detail as possible to find a note in a list or gallery view. Evernote doesn't have a part or page structure; each notebook only has pages; there is no way to divide notebooks into sections.

When we return to our physical notebooks, we scribble everything on the following blank page since we cannot quickly go over those notes and organize them by category. This method of notetaking, which is sequential regardless of the topic, does not help us when looking for all the samples that meet the same criteria or all the information on one subject.

Cross-platform: You can utilize OneNote on any computer, phone, or tablet because it is cross-platform. Since all of these devices have access to the same notes, you can finish taking notes on your computer and then view them on your phone while away from the office. OneNote is accessible from anywhere. Additionally, OneNote allows you to sync locally with any of your devices so that you can access your notes even when there is no internet connection.

The Notes app on the iPhone is simple, but it does not offer a local synced copy for your PC. The iPhone Notes app will sync with your iCloud preferences and give you access to your notes via the web browser on your PC. Even though the free edition allows you to sync two locations, Evernote lets you access your notes from various devices. Even though a regular notebook is portable, you can only access the most recent entries (unless you want to take along your entire collection of notebooks!). Additionally, you risk leaving your notebook at home or losing it altogether.

Keeping everything in one place: Staying organized can be easier using OneNote as your digital notebook. In addition to your notes, you'll have access to pictures and movies with integrated audio, emails, documents, weblinks, web clippings, schematics, and much more.

All of this information will also be accessible to others if you share your notebook with them. For instance, you might want to share notebooks with your team when working on projects or committees as a group. Sharing for personal use could be useful when planning a trip with friends or a big occasion like a wedding or anniversary party. Here are some other considerations:

The Apple Notes app allows you to add images, documents, and drawings, but seeing them requires an iPad or phone, and note sharing is limited. Even while Evernote stores all of your notes in one area, unless you upgrade to the premium edition, you won't have access to them on all of your devices (keep in mind that you can only have two locations with the free Evernote app). Furthermore, there is no way to interface with Microsoft products. For instance, the Team connection is not accessible unless you purchase Evernote Professional.

A paper notebook could burst with loose papers, earmarks, highlights, and other distinctive markings, and it might also be filled to the brim with individuality. This approach, though, could grow cumbersome and isn't always the best course of action (as we may be missing the meeting agenda or other supporting documents that we still have to refer to on our digital devices).

Using OneNote as your notebook gives you the benefits of organization, searchability, and accessibility to your notes and media from anywhere, at any time. You can access your OneNote notebook from any device and store all your information because it is digital.

If you need to gather information for either personal or professional reasons, OneNote is the answer.

The interface

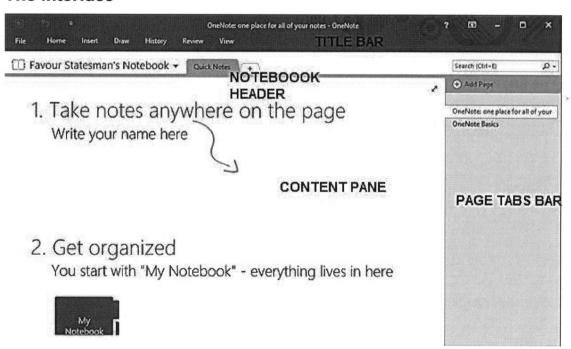

The OneNote interface presented when you first open the program is depicted above. When you initially use OneNote, the application creates an example notebook named **Personal**. When you use the program again in the future, the last notebook you worked on will open instead.

The storage structure of OneNote is similar to that of a tabbed notebook. The beauty of OneNote is that you may tailor the organization to your preferences and requirements. One notebook for personal information and another for business, for example. Alternatively, you may keep a separate notebook for each project you work on. Each area of your notebook is split into pages, and each page is divided into sections.

The notebook information shows four parts of the OneNote interface once the program and notebook are active. At the top of the program window, the Notebook Drop-Down Navigation displays buttons for the notebooks you create. You choose a notebook to work on from the drop-down menu.

Notebooks were previously shown in a collapsed Notebook window on the left side of the OneNote interface. You may access and show the previous navigation by clicking the pin button in the notebook drop-down. This is the same button that is used to close the Notebook window.

The Navigation Bar is default collapsible, revealing a button for each notebook. Selecting one of these buttons in the Navigation Bar may quickly navigate between notebooks. The contents of the notebooks may be collapsed and expanded by clicking the little downward-pointing arrows. Then, inside the notebook, select any of these places to get to that part easily.

The current notebook page is shown in the **"Content"** window in the middle of the OneNote interface. The page's name is shown in the Title Bar at the top of the OneNote interface for pages you create.

The Notebook Header is located just above the Content" window and shows tabs for the current notebook's sections. You may quickly go to various notebook parts by clicking these tabs.

The **Page Tabs Bar** appears to the right of the **"Content"** pane and displays page tabs that you may click to navigate between the current section's pages quickly. OneNote default creates a tab for each page in the current section.

The **Ribbon** is a new item displayed at the top of the OneNote interface. This is where you'll find all of the program's tabs, button groups, and commands. If you're acquainted with Ribbon, one thing to keep in mind is that, unlike other Office apps, OneNote's Ribbon is folded by default. This allows for additional room on notebook pages. The Ribbon appears when you click a tab. You may access the **"Backstage View"** shared by Microsoft Office programs by selecting the **"File"** option in the Ribbon. The most frequent file management operations, such as creating a new notebook, sharing notebooks, and printing, are found under the **"Backstage View."**

The Quick Access Toolbar is located above the Ribbon. You may quickly add buttons to this toolbar for the commands you use the most and want to have accessible at all times. Several crucial buttons, such as **"Back"** and **"Undo,"** have already been put here. You may quickly delete the buttons you've placed on this toolbar.

You'll notice a cleaner, more modern interface if you update a previous version of OneNote. You can use OneNote without a keyboard since they support touch-enabled devices.

Use the **"Touch/Mouse Mode"** button to increase the spacing between buttons in the Ribbon, making it simpler to choose items with your fingertips. Add the "Touch/Mouse" button to the Quick Access Toolbar to switch between modes quickly.

To do so, go to the Quick Access Toolbar and click or press the drop-down arrow. Then, in the toolbar, choose **"Touch/Mouse Mode."** Then pick the desired mode by tapping or clicking the **"Touch/Mouse Mode"** button on the Quick Access Toolbar.

Book 5: - Access

This section deals with the basic elements you must know when working with Access. It is the beginning aspect of working with access, and therefore you shouldn't take this section for granted because it is the determinant factor of how far you can go with Access. It involves the description of the Access database, indispensable database terminology, database object, and a database file. Let's get started with the reason why you need to use Access.

WHY DO YOU HAVE TO USE ACCESS?

The main purpose of using Access is to help you to store large arrays of data, arrange the data and retrieve the data when it is needed. Some users thought Access and Excel serve the same purpose far, be it storing data in Excel is limited to the number of rows in Excel worksheet and can only help you to sort and filter a minor list of data. Still, Access deals with compound and bulky data arrays beyond what Excel can do or try to do.

WHAT IS AN ACCESS DATABASE?

A database can also be called a database file. It is an organized collection of an item that relates to specific information, and the item can be anything, such as a product, employee name, etc. For instance, Amazon is a database with organized items you can purchase, and the items contain attached information such as name, price, author, title, and many more. Another example of a database is a library catalog with an organized collection of information about books.

A MUST-KNOW (10) TERMINOLOGY FOR MASTERING ACCESS DATABASE

It is expedient to understand the basic term of access database to understand in and out of the database. The table below explains 10 database terminology you must recognize if you run the access database conveniently.

THE NEEDED 10 DATABASE TERMINOLOGY YOU NEED TO KNOW	
Database	This is an orderly method of organizing information for easy retrieval when it is needed for any purpose.
Database table	It is referred to the orderly arrangement of data information into fields (columns) and records (rows).
Fields	It can be likened to a column in a conventional table, the categories of information inside the database table.

Records	It can be likened to a row in a conventional table, showing all the recorded data about each category, whether of a person or anything.
Cells	Like a conventional table, a cell is the intersection of field and record inside a database. It is the point where you can enter a piece of data
Foreign key or field	It links information in database tables, i.e., it shows the relationship between two database tables by relating it with the primary key. The unique column compared with another column during comparison is known as a primary key.
Primary key field	This is a field in each database table whose values uniquely identify other fields across the table.
Relational database	This is the type of database where data is stored in more than one database table. It helps to organize data into a table that can be related together based on the fact that data must be common to each other, for instance, a company that recorded the first database table with customer details and another database describing individual customer transactions. The database used to have more than one database table, but a situation may warrant that it will have only one database; in such a situation, it is called a flat-file database.
Dynaset	It refers to taking data or a set of data in one or more database tables, i.e., the outcome of your search within the database.
Object	The object comprises various components in constructing a database, such as database tables, queries, forms, reports, macros, and modules. They will be discussed at length later in this section.

COMPOSITION OF DATABASE OBJECT

Database objects consist of all the elements that allow you to enter, store, analyze, compile and extract your data the way you want. There are many numbers of an object, but we will focus on the main objects, which are Tables, queries, forms, reports, macros, and modules, as I have mentioned in the database terminology. Without these components, you can't effectively operate the database, and I will quickly discuss them one after the other below.

USING TABLES TO STORE DATABASE DATA

A database table is the database component where related information is stored in **fields (columns)** and **records (rows).** A table can store all information in a field, such as a Supplier ID, employee Name, Contact Address, Position, and so on, but each table must contain related information. The record must contain information that relates to the field.

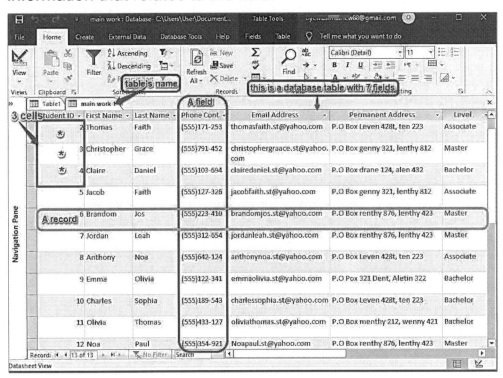

Generally speaking, a database used to have more than one database table; nevertheless, when the information is not large, you may use only one database table.

GENERATING FORMS TO ENTER AND MAINTAIN DATABASE DATA

The next action after creating the table is to enter data into respective fields and records. The Forms help you to enter, edit, view, and delete data. In short, form is used to create data and as well use to create data and as well use to carry all forms of data manipulation such as editing, viewing, modifying, and many more. However, you have the choice to enter and modify data straightway without a form, but it won't be as easier compared to a form.

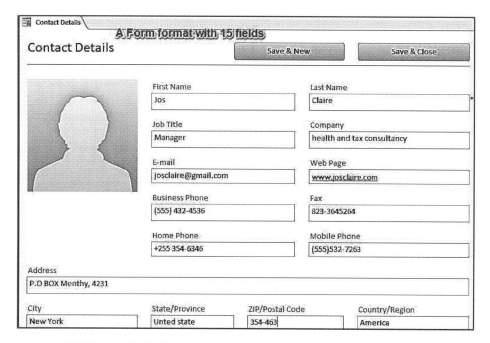

SELECTING QUERIES TO EXTRACT DATABASE DATA

A query is designed to extract specified information that you want to work with from the table. The query is used to sort and filter the data based on the search criteria. Query means passing a question to your database by defining specific search criteria based on the needed information. For instance, you may say who customer care is. In this case, you are asking your database to find your customer care under the job title category.

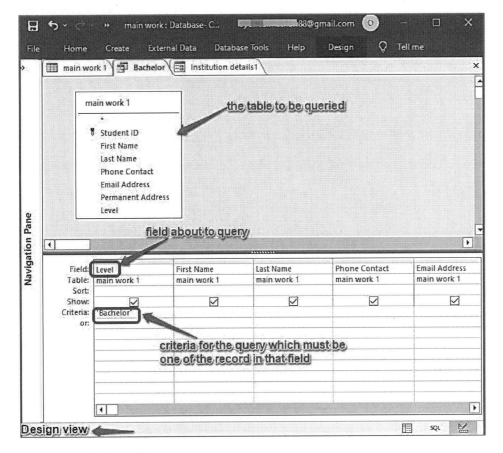

Result of the above query

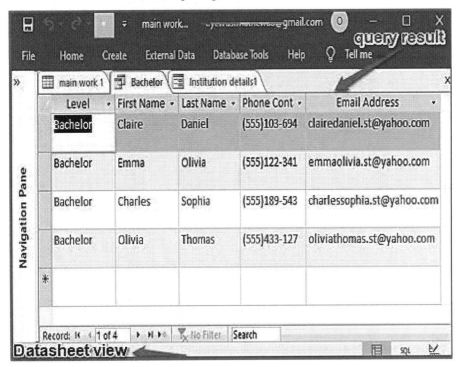

USING REPORTS FOR DATA PRESENTATION AND INSPECTION

Reports are usually an output result from the selected queries or tables, and reports are always on paper in printed format, which is meant to be presented to higher or recognized authorities for proper inspection and scrutinization.

ID	Payment date	First Name	Last Name	Faculties
List of students with late payment registration			Monday, 6 sept, 2021	
-1936620916	20/02/2020			
		Anthony	Noa	Commerce
162990325	20/09/2020			
		Jos	Claire	Arts
580430464	05/05/2020			
		Claire	Daniel	Educations
1499693350	23/09/2020			
		Brandom	Jos	Education
1630387005	31/12/2020			
		Thomas	Faith	Science
1630407387	04/11/2020			
		Christopher	Grace	Economics

MACRO

Macro is simply a programming language invented by Microsoft for creating instructions and commands in the form. Using Macro extends what you can do with Microsoft Access. For instance, you can add a button to the form for opening another related form or report, which will introduce a wizard to guide you with the command, but you can only do it once. Nevertheless, Macro can repeatedly help you achieve such a command with a drop-down list, and macro can help you to open an executive query and view and print reports. The limiting factor of Macro is that you can't make any choice outside the command within the drop-down list.

MODULE

The module is designed to help you store VBA code, either the code you wrote or available on Microsoft Wizard Access. The module works as a macro, but the Module permits you to write your code without any limitations depending on your skill and language. Still, Macro is limited depending on the command writer by Microsoft Access available on the drop-down list.

SHORTCUTS AND CONTROL KEYS

The following are the essential shortcuts you need to commit to the memory to help you with the Access task quickly.

SHORTCUTS FOR ENTERING DATA IN DATASHEET VIEW

Keyboard Shortcuts	Destination
↓	Moving to the next record of the same field
↑	Moving to the previous record of the same field
Enter or Tab or right arrow	Moving to the next field in the same record.
Shift + Tab or right arrow	Moving to the previous field in the same record.
Home	Moving to the first field of the current record.
End	Moving to the last field of the current record.
Ctrl + Home	Moving to the first field in the first record.
Ctrl + End	Moving to the last field in the last record.
Page up	Moving up one screen.
Page down	Moving down one screen.

GENERAL SHORTCUTS

Keyboard shortcuts	Purposes
Ctrl + O	Open an existing database
F11	Show/ hide navigation pane
F2	Switch between edit mode navigation mode in datasheet and design view
F1	Open the Help window
Ctrl + F1	Expand/collapse the ribbon
Ctrl + S	Save the database objects
Ctrl + X	Move the selected content into the clipboard
Ctrl + C	Copy the selected content into the clipboard

Ctrl + V	Paste the clipboard content into the selected cells or sections.
Ctrl + F	Open Find in find and replace dialog box in both views
Ctrl + H	Open Replace in the find and replace dialog box in both views.

GRID PANE SHORTCUTS

Keyboard shortcuts	Purposes
Arrow keys, Tab key, shift + tab keys	To move among cells
Ctrl + Spacebar	To select an entire grid column
F2	To switch between edit mode and navigation mode
Ctrl + X	Move the selected content into the clipboard
Ctrl + C	Copy the selected content into the clipboard
Ctrl + V	Paste the clipboard content into the selected cells or sections.
Ctrl + Home	Moving to the first field in the first record.
Ctrl + End	Moving to the last field in the last record.

Book 6: - Outlook

GETTING STARTED WITH OUTLOOK

Microsoft Outlook comes in different flavors compared to other Microsoft Office applications. The Interface is a bit varied from other Offices' interfaces, and it has a separate App button that will link you to various tasks you can execute with Outlook. The Interface includes the "**App Bar,**" which comprises various app buttons for executing diverse tasks on Microsoft Outlook.

A click on any of the **app buttons** on the App Bar will lead you to separate windows for carrying out the corresponding tasks of the selected app.

DISTINGUISHED FUNCTIONS OF MICROSOFT OUTLOOK

Microsoft Outlook is aimed to help you in the following areas:

1. **Email Container**: this is the Outlook section designed for sending and receiving email messages, documents, and files. It has systemic features of arranging email messages into a distinct folder to monitor the flow of email messages.

2. **Event Scheduler**: you can use this area to schedule a meeting, event, outing, and appointment. You need to state when and where the meeting or events will occur; Outlook will carry out the remaining activities. You will get to know more about Scheduler as we proceed.

3. **The Address Register**: This section deals with storing and keeping contact and email addresses of relatives, friends, and families.

4. **Reminder App**: this area will wake you up for the forthcoming events. All you need to do is to program each of your forthcoming events and meetings.

5. **Jotters**: there is an additional benefit of using Outlook. It gives you the privilege of jotting down important information for future reference.

GETTING ACQUAINTED WITH THE OUTLOOK APPLICATION

You've not yet known what Outlook is capable of doing until you get familiar with the position and function of each application. I have explained the function of each application in the preceding section, while the position of each app is described in the image below:

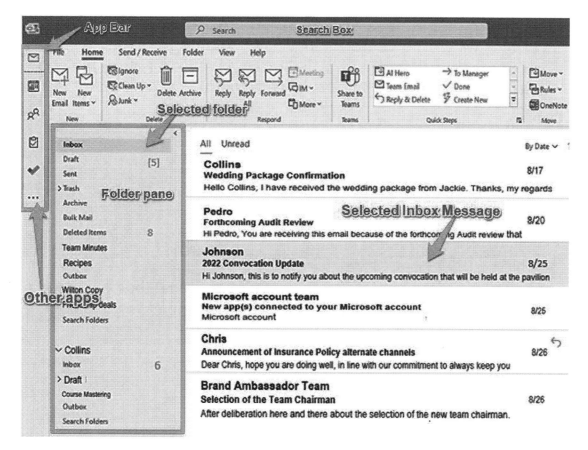

Note: you can click on any applications from the App Bar to run the corresponding program, such as **Mail, Calendar, People, Tasks, and Notes.**

Tip: sometimes, the folder Pane may not be visible. All you need to do to make it visible is to click on the **"View"** tab, tap on the **"Folder Pane"** menu and place a checkmark on the Normal from the drop-down list.

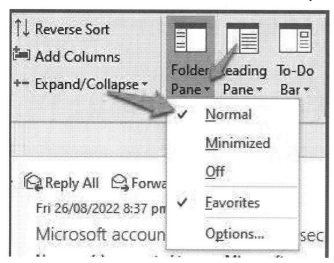

WORKING WITH CATEGORIES

Navigating and finding items in a folder may seem laborious if you fail to categorize the items within the Folder, especially if the concerned Folder has multiple items. When you categorize your folder items finding any of the items becomes easier. Let me explain what categories mean. It means assigning a code color to the items for easy recognition within a folder.

However, certain Outlook emails are not supported for categorizing items. Thus if you are using such an email, you may find it difficult to categorize items of such email, for instance, IMAP email.

CREATING A CATEGORY

The first assignment for organizing folder items is to create a category. The following are the processes for creating categories:

    i. Open the concerned Folder and select the **"Item"** that you want to assign with a new category, such as an email message or a contact.

    ii. Tap the **Home** tab and click on **Categorize** menu, then select **All Categories** from the drop-down menu to access the Color Categories dialog box.

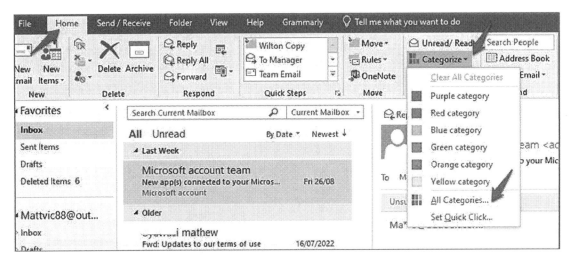

    iii. Using the Color Categories dialog box, you have two options either to create a new category or remodel any color categories as shown below:

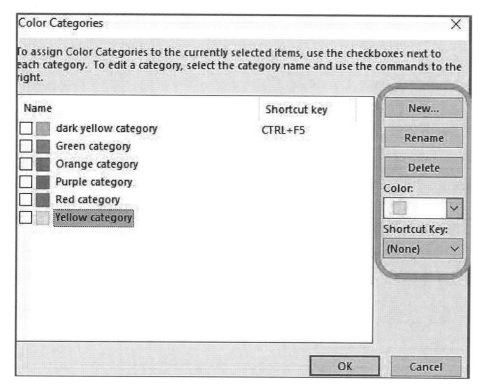

a. **Create a self-category**: tap over the **New** button to access the "**Add New Category**" dialog box. Insert a new name for the category you want to create and click the **Color** menu to select the color from the color drop-down menu. You may click on the **Shortcut Key** menu to select a shortcut that you will use to assign the new categories to the items and finally tap on the **Ok** button to authenticate the process.

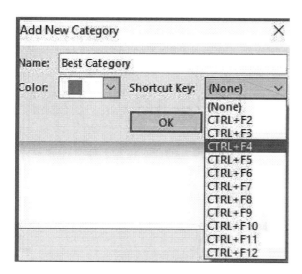

b. **Remodeling a category**: select any available color categories you want to reconstruct and click the Rename button, enter a different **color name**, choose a different **color** from the color menu and select the **shortcut key** for assigning the color category from the shortcut drop-down menu.

Note: you can delete a category by selecting the category in the **Color Categories** dialog box and tapping over the **Delete** button. Though the color category will be erased, the items will still retain the category identity.

ASSIGNING FOLDERS ITEMS TO DESIRE CATEGORIES

At this level, you must have gotten enough color categories, both the categories you created and the prefabricated categories. Then we can proceed further to assign a category to any folder item of your choice by following the itemized steps:

i. Open the concerned Folder and select the **item** you want to assign to the color category.

ii. Tap over the **Home** tab, click the categorize menu and select the desired **category** for the selected item.

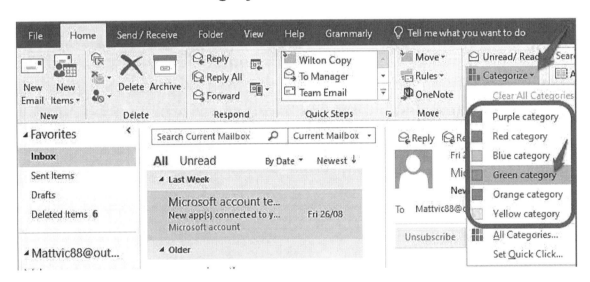

Note: if you select the shortcut key for the color categories you want to select, you can quickly press the **Ctrl key + that key** to assign such color categories to the selected item, or you can also right-click the selected **Item**, then tap on the **Categorize** menu and select the color **category** from the shortcut menu.

If you wish to clear a category, kindly select the item with the category, tap over the Home tab, click on the Categories menu, and **select Clear All Categories** from the drop-down menu.

SEARCHING FOR THE LOST ITEMS IN A FOLDER

Perhaps you have done all you could to find a particular item in a folder but all to no avail; whether by changing the sorting arrangement, view arrangement, or by scrolling up and down, then what you are expected to do in such a situation is to search by making use of the **Search Box** to locate any missing items such as **mail, contact, appointment, and tasks**. The next section explains various ways of running a search on Microsoft Outlook.

Suppose you have searched items before; you can revisit those search items by clicking on the Recent menu and selecting any of your previous search items from the drop-down menu. When you are done searching, click on Close Search to return to the main windows, where you can see the contents of the selected Folder.

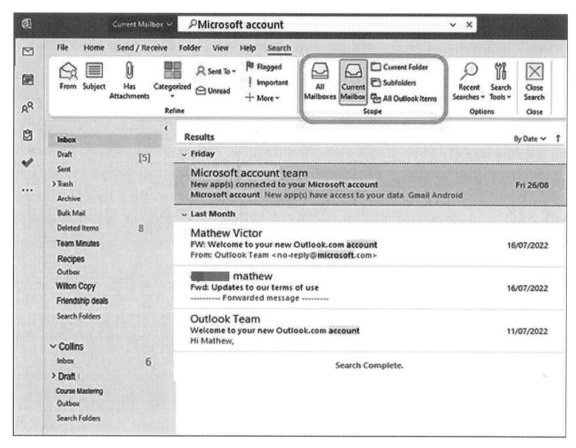

RUNNING AN INSTANT SEARCH

An instant search is a process of inserting a keyword into the search box to search for specific items on the selected Folder. As you begin typing the keyword into the Search box, the corresponding items will be displayed and highlighted on the search result.

Outlook will recommend as many as possible results that correspond with your keyword search. Kindly click any of the suggestions to check what you are searching for.

Nevertheless, you can adjust Instant Search options by moving to the Search bar and clicking on the **Search Tools** menu, then selecting the **Search option** from the drop-down menu to access the "**Outlook Options**" dialog box. Select

Search Category and adjust Instant Search options such as folder selection for your search and how you want your search result to be arranged.

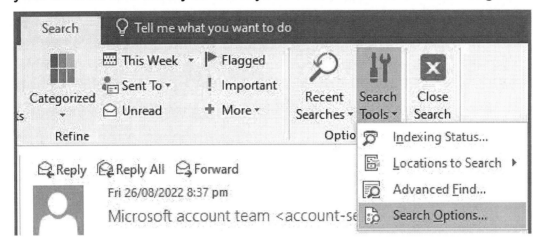

REFINING YOUR SEARCH

This is applicable after you have run a search and you are provided with multiple results to the extent that you don't know which one you are looking for. In such a case, Refining a search is the answer. You can refine your search by modifying the scope of your search and selecting refine options.

MODIFYING THE SCOPE OF YOUR SEARCH

The scope of your search is the area your search result will cover, and you can either expand or narrow your search with the search you pick. The following explains the type of your scope search as they are shown in the Scope section:

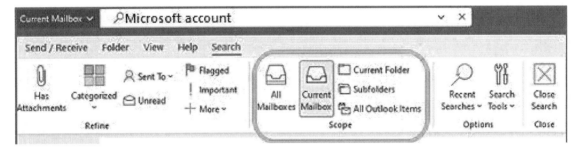

❖ **Current Folder**: this limits your search results to the Folder selected on the Folder Window.

❖ **Subfolders**: this extends your search results coverage by including the selected folder's subfolders.

❖ **Current Mailbox**: this option extends your search result to all the folder items that contain emails of the particular address you are running for those who configure more than one mail address (it applies to email alone).

❖ **All Mailboxes**: this option extends your search results to all the folder items that contain emails of all email addresses you configured to the Outlook program (it applies to email alone).

❖ **All Outlook items**: this option covers the search results of all the Outlook folders. You can place a mouse over any search results to see the Folder where such an item is stored.

USING REFINE OPTIONS

Refine options are typically used to limit the extent of your search results using the selected refine option. Move to the **Refine** group on the "**Search**" tab and click over any refine options to narrow down your result. The available option in the Refine group is subject to the selected Folder you are searching, such as Email, People, calendar, and so on.

For instance, you can search for the emails you have gotten from a specific individual by selecting "**From**" from the refine option and entering the Sender name to get all the emails received from such a person or "**Subject**" to search for a particular email by typing the keyword subject of such an email after selecting Subject from the Refine Options.

CONDUCTING THOROUGH SEARCH USING ADVANCED FIND OPTION

Have you tried all the above search options and still not gotten the desired search result? You can conduct a thorough search using the Advanced Find option.

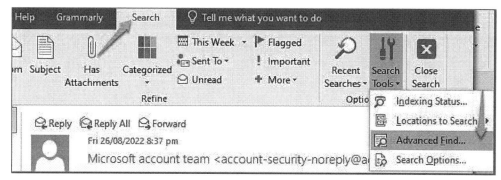

To make use of the Advance Find option, kindly:

❖ Click on the **Search Tools** menu and select the **Advanced Find** button on the drop-down menu on the Search tab.

❖ The "**Advanced Find**" dialog box will come forth. Enter the word you are finding to the "**Search for the word (s)**" box and click over the **Browse** button to access the "**Select Folder(s)**" dialog box.

❖ Then select one or more folders where the word(s) you want to get can be found and click **Ok** to return to the "**Advanced Find**" dialog box.

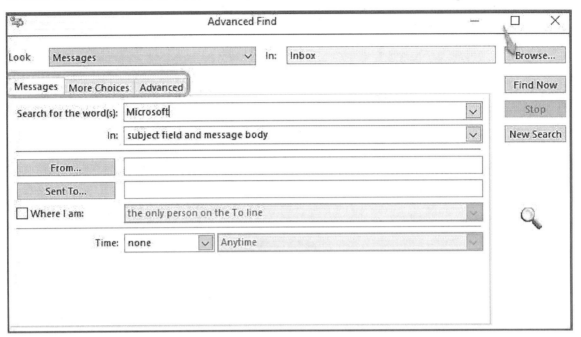

Note: You can use the three tabs at the top of the "Search for the word(s) section to specify your search area. However, the options of the three tabs always vary based on the selected Folder you want to search.

DELETING OUTLOOK ITEMS(EMAIL MESSAGES, PEOPLE, AND SO ON)

The more you receive email messages, store contacts, and perform other tasks on Outlook, the more it fills up. When much information fills up Outlook, it will be congested, and this makes it necessary to remove any information that is not needed anymore to create enough space for the present and future information. You can use any of these two options to send out the information that is not relevant anymore:

❖ Right-click the offending **Items** and select **Delete** from the shortcuts menu.

❖ Select the offending **Item** and press the **Delete** button on the keyboard.

Note: each of the deleted items will be dropped into the **Deleted Items folder**, allowing you to restore them when required. However, when you have decided to erase an item from Outlook memory, you can go to the **Deleted Items folder** to delete such an item forever.

Tip: you can empty the Deleted Items folder by right-clicking **Deleted Item** folder and selecting the **Empty Folder** from the shortcut menu.

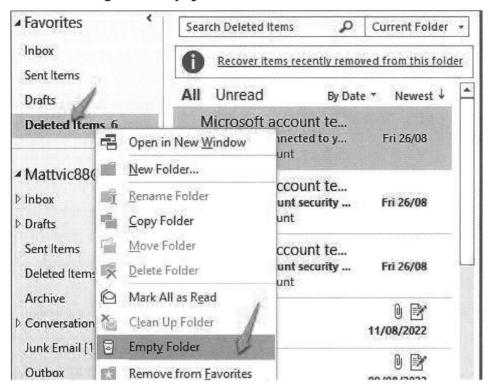

Note: To restore the deleted item, right-click such **Item** inside the Deleted Items Folder and select **Move**, then specify where that item came from to send it back to its previous location.

Book 7: - Teams

Microsoft Teams is a collaboration platform where you can chat, share documents, have online meetings, and other useful features for business collaboration, online learning, teamwork, *etc.*

It has many features that you can utilize for your use. You can schedule classes, hold classes, write on a virtual board, sit in classrooms, *etc.* The only difference it'd have with the learning you are accustomed to is that it is virtual.

Students, faculty, teachers, educators, and staff can meet, interact, learn, create content, share content, and collaborate using Microsoft Teams on Office 365 Education. Distance, the pandemic, and other restrictions are no longer barriers to effective communication with this effective collaboration platform.

Microsoft is adding many new features and applications to Office 365, such as Planner, Shift, and Microsoft Teams.

Teams is a collaboration app with all your chats and conversations, your meetings, and all your files in one location. With Teams, you can communicate and collaborate in a single and secure location. You get a messaging platform, online meeting, calling capabilities, live collaboration on files, native integration with office apps, but also integration to many non-office apps that you're currently using.

To understand what you can do with Teams and how it could allow you to collaborate more effectively, you need to be ready to practice as you go.

Installing Microsoft Teams

Go to "teams.microsoft.com" in any software and log in with your Microsoft account. On the off occasion that you don't already have one, you can create one for free.

Once you have signed into your Microsoft account, click to download and install the application on your Windows, iOS, macOS, Linux-powered device, or Android device.

Although the program-based web application version does not support ongoing meetings or conferences, there are times when using a program to access Teams is speedier. Click "Utilize the Web App Instead" to access Teams from your software rather than downloading the application.

You might need to re-sign in when the Teams application is first installed on your device. After there, to begin creating your association, select "Pursue Teams."

You'll be taken to another website page where you may read a complete summary of the highlights and consider comparing strategies. If you use Groups alone and don't use any other Microsoft Office 365 applications, it's free.

If you're joining an existing organization, choose "Utilizing Teams already? Log In" You'll be ready to look into your association's current Teams architecture and start communicating with your partners once you sign in.

If you are beginning another association, click "Sign Up for Free."

Enter your email and afterward select "Next."

Enter your first and last name just as the name of your organization or association. At the point when there is no doubt about it, "Set Up Teams."

You and your associates would now be able to work together distantly through this association in Microsoft Teams. You can fabricate a superior correspondence stage by making new groups inside your association, incorporating Teams with Office 365, and sharing your screen, your records, or your preferred feline pictures.

Microsoft Teams as a Mobile & Desktop Application

Microsoft is quickly developing its Teams application on iOS and Android, as the cooperation instrument grasps first line and other portable specialists.

There has been something of an ocean change at Microsoft in recent years. It used to be an organization centered around gifted 'information laborers, with the trademark 'A PC on each work area and in each home.' The statement of purpose is currently 'to engage each individual and each association on the planet to accomplish more.' With the difference in accentuation from PCs to individuals, there is a move to supporting first-line laborers, who regularly work moves and are typically paid continuously.

If there is one thing that the Teams versatile application is not, it is a clone of the work area Teams understanding. While that would be simple for Microsoft to convey, it would not be the simple-to-utilize, simple-to-learn application that a first-line laborer requires. They should have the option to get it and get the opportunity to work with negligible preparation. So, the portable Teams should be intended to work like some other iPhone or Android application, with a natural look-and-believe and support for versatile local highlights.

Teams include that bode well on portable, while others are there to assist you with dealing with your work/life balance more viable. That can be as straightforward as setting calm occasions to shut out calls and messages when you prefer not to be upset. Dissimilar to Windows' Focus Assist instruments,

Teams offers an alternative of Quiet Days, which permit you to shut out entire days - halting warnings at the ends of the week or moving rest days.

One significant component in the portable rendition of Teams is Walkie Talkie, propelling on Android gadgets in July. Like the old press-to-talk telephones, it is a method to immediately place staff in contact with one another. Utilizing Wi-Fi or cell information, it gives a secure voice correspondence channel for people and gatherings. Walkie Talkie is a piece of Microsoft's organization with Samsung's cell phone gathering, with the new Galaxy XCover Pro tough telephone offering an equipment 'talk' button that enacts the element.

Walkie Talkie resembles any Teams application and should be introduced from the Teams administrator focus. When presented and conveyed to gadgets, you will have to set up committed groups and channels for Walkie-Talkie to fragment gatherings of clients and maintain a strategic distance from crosstalk and disarray. Clients will interface with a chain when they. Please move and disengage when they leave.

Firmly related is a simple method of sharing your area and guiding it into your gadget's current GPS and planning apparatuses. Tap on the '... 'In a talk, where you typically pick an emoticon or connection to video transfers, and Teams will embed a guide bit and a location. It is a valuable path for field administration engineers or other versatile specialists to immediately tell others where they are according to current calls, making it more straightforward to rapidly distribute assignments to the laborer closest to a call.

Microsoft is unmistakably mindful of the contrasts between work areas and portable use. A portion of the versatile Team's highlights ensures that utilizing Teams does not take away from your gadget's look and feel. That incorporates support for a dim mode, which can be helpful in low-light conditions or prefer not to upset the individuals around you. Different choices simplify tweaking the catches and menus, so you can have the instruments and applications you use inside Teams right where you need them.

Present-day cell phones are more than versatile PCs; they are ground-breaking cameras also. Microsoft's ML-controlled Office Lens is an instrument for taking and sharing pictures of records and screens, cutting undesirable fringes, and altering points of view. It transforms a telephone into a versatile scanner, and by incorporating Office Lens into the portable Teams application, you can rapidly share paper records with partners without leaving the app.

Setting Up Microsoft Teams

First, go to your Start menu, then to "*Settings,*" and navigate to "*Accounts*". Go to the tab that says "Access work or school account," and if you have any of these accounts linked to your device, you will see them here.

Next, double-click to open Teams. You will get a welcome screen asking you to pick an account to continue. These accounts are already linked to the device, and the number of accounts linked to your device will be displayed here. Select an account to proceed. This will link that account to Microsoft Teams, and whenever you open Teams, it will automatically log in with that account.

If you follow this step, you may not be asked to enter a password during this process because your account has already been linked to this device. This means your password has also been linked and synchronized with Microsoft 365, so it is more like a single sign-in, and you wouldn't be asked to sign in with your password.

However, whenever you change your password from office 365, then Teams would require you to enter your new password.

As technology continues to advance, life gets better with Microsoft Teams. This is because the Teams keep advancing with the inclusion of new features making connectivity possible between people in different parts of the world.

Microsoft Teams is an effective way of making the internet a learning atmosphere for students. Instructors can make use of this tool to schedule and hold meetings on the internet with students across the globe without any problem at all.

Furthermore, teachers who have urgent projects to assign to their students and do not have the opportunity to meet with them physically can use Microsoft Teams to carry on with the activities. Besides that, instructors can share the documents they'll need with the students. Teachers can start a meeting with the students by connecting to a web app or the Teams desktop client.

Setting Up Your Account

The first step to using the Microsoft Teams application is registering an account with Microsoft. Individuals who already have an account registered with Microsoft, either from Skype or any other Microsoft application, do not have a problem and can move on to signing up. But if you haven't had a registration or used any of Microsoft's applications, you will have to create a unified account that can be used to access other offers from Microsoft.

After registering an account with Microsoft, you have to go to your TEAMS app or the web version to sign up with Teams.

TEAMS on website

TEAMS on the Desktop app

Click on the signup button, which will lead you to an opt-in page where you have to input your Microsoft user account information to continue or any other email of your choice. Type in your email and click Next.

 Microsoft

Enter an email

We'll use this email to set up Teams. If you already have a Microsoft account, feel free to use that email here.

someone@example.com

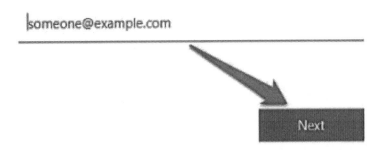

Next up, you have to clarify what use your TEAMS application is for. Be it for your office, home, or school. Choose and click next

NOTE: Selecting Teams for Friends and family will direct you to sign up with skype because TEAMS was created for the workplace and school. So if you indeed want a video conference application just for getting together with friends and family, then Microsoft will suggest you use Skype instead.

After selecting For work or school, you will be asked to put a password for your account and then fill up information about your full name, company name, and Nationality. Fill in the information correctly and click set up teams.

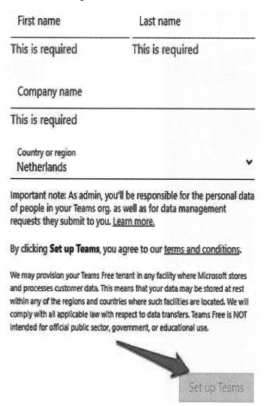

After which, you will be asked to download the TEAMS app or use the web version.

But if you already have the downloaded application on your phone or desktop, you will see a tab that pops up like this.

Open Microsoft Teams?

https://teams.microsoft.com wants to open this application.

Open Microsoft Teams   Cancel

You will then be signed in to the Microsoft Teams platform, regardless of the version you chose, web, mobile or desktop app. Click Continue

As simple as that, you would have made your way to the home page of Microsoft Teams, where you would be given a link you can share with your contacts or via emails so that they can join your organization.

Following the steps above would have enabled you to set up your TEAMS completely account from signup to sign in. Let's move on.

Note: Be sure to remember the information used to sign up for Microsoft Teams, as that information will be required to fill in if you are attempting to sign in on another device, thus meaning your information can be used to sign in on any other device giving you the mobility to use TEAMS across devices.

Setting up Video Conferencing in Microsoft Teams

Click on "Gatherings" on the left-hand side of the screen. You can either plan a gathering or start one right away. For the last mentioned, select "Meet Now." You will be given the alternative to name your audience and flip your sound and video on or off. Snap "Join now" when you are prepared. At the base, from left to right, these permit you to flip your camera on or off, switch your mic on or off, share your screen, get to more alternatives, lift your hand, see the visit, view members, or hang up. Click the three specks in the center to get extra options like entering full screen, empowering live inscriptions, or turning off video for members who join the call. When the gathering begins, you may get a spring-up window with two choices for adding individuals to the call: you can either get a connection to share or send an email welcome. If you do not get this window naturally or need to get to it later, click on the "Show members" button on the right side of the catch line. At that point, in the sidebar on the right, click on the "Offer Invitation" catch to open that equivalent window.

New members who utilize your connection to join the gathering will initially hold up in a virtual entryway and be told, "Somebody in the gathering should give you access soon." If you are facilitating the audience, when their name appears in the "Individuals" sidebar, click on the checkmark close to their name to add them to the call. If you haven't empowered the sidebar, you will get a little spring-up window over the "Show members" button at the base of the screen to caution you that they're pausing; click "Concede" to add them to the call.

To schedule a meeting for another time. Click on "Meetings" on the left-hand sidebar.

Click the "Calendar a meeting" button.

A window will spring up, letting you set the time and date for the gathering alongside a title. Click "Timetable" when you are set.

The following box will give you the alternative to "Duplicate gathering greeting" to get a connection to join the gathering. You can likewise consequently share your welcome using Google Calendar and Microsoft Outlook, contingent upon what administrations you are at present marked into.

Also, that is it! Since your gathering is unique, you will have the option to sign onto it whenever, yet along these lines, you and different members will make some planned memories to meet.

Join Meeting on Microsoft Teams

Various approaches exist to access and join a gathering in Teams, including through connection, telephone, schedule, station, or talk.

Joining with a Link

Click the link given in your Teams meeting invitation. Your meeting will consequently open in Teams.

Otherwise, you can click on the Join Microsoft Teams Meeting directly.

The meeting invite records a telephone number and meeting ID. At that point, you can join that meeting by Phone.

Joining by Phone

The meeting may be joined by phone, and the invite will list toll and a toll-free phone number. You can choose both numbers, contingent upon your necessities and inclinations.

Dial the suitable phone number.

Enter the meeting ID when incited.

The greeting will likewise have a rundown of nearby numbers to choose from. You can select a telephone number from this rundown; instead, if the cost and complimentary telephone numbers are not neighborhood to you.

Joining your MS Teams Calendar

To join a Teams meeting from your schedule,

Choose the Calendar from the menu on the left-hand side of the page.

Click any picture on this page to see it at full size.

From your schedule, click on the meeting you wish to join. A window will show up with a Join button.

Click Join.

Creating a channel

Click on the ellipse to the right of the team name.

Click Add Channel.

Enter the channel's name and a description of the channel's purpose.

(Optional) Click the Privacy drop-down menu to specify whether your channel is only visible to you or public to your team.

Click Add.

Each member of your team has access to the channels you create, but they will be hidden in the list of the channel that your team members have. If you are your team's owner, you have the additional option to Show this channel automatically on everyone's list, which adds it to the default list for each member.

Joining by Channel

Channels are MS Teams' subsets; they empower colleagues to hold discussions and offer records about discrete undertakings that do not require all colleagues' cooperation. You can also join a Teams meeting from a channel, and the gathering will incorporate the member recorded in the circuit.

Click on the Join button to join a Teams meeting through a channel.

Teams Navigation buttons

The TEAMS navigation buttons are a tiny productivity trick that is incredibly easy to overlook. As seen in the Figure Below, you can use this feature to move ahead and backward, just like your browser's forward and back buttons. However, the web edition of TEAMS does not offer this capability.

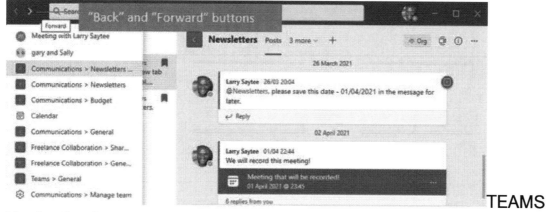TEAMS

Navigation buttons and history

Book 8: - Publisher

Whenever you launch Publisher, you will find several available templates. Meanwhile, to create a publication, you should choose a template you want to look like.

Once you launch the template, you then have the chance to change it to contain elements like fonts, graphics, and colors.

Using a template to create a publication

Users can explore templates installed with Publisher to create amazing publications.

Here's how:

1. Select **File and New**.
2. Choose a type of publication in the template gallery list, like Thank you cards.
3. Then with your right and left arrows, carefully scroll through different designs and locate the template you like.
4. Finally, select the option to **Create**.

Saving a publication as a template

You can also create a template from a publication by saving the publication as a Publisher template file.

Here's how:

1. Open or create the publication you would like to utilize as a template.
2. Select **File and Save As**, and check through the list to the C drive on your PC.
3. While around the Save as type field, choose **Publisher Template**.
4. Also, while in the File name field, enter a template name.
5. Select **Save**.

Changing a template

To change an already existing template, you should follow the steps below:

1. Select **File and New**.

2. *Also, select Personal and double-click the template name **(NB: If you fail to see your template name, it means you are yet to save it in the default template location folder)**.*

3. Once you have found and selected the template name, proceed to make the necessary alterations you like for the template.

4. Then select File and Save As, and navigate to the C drive on your PC.

5. Move over to the Save as type field, select Publisher Template, and enter a new name and elective category for the template.

6. Finally, select Save.

Troubleshooting common Office 365

During your journey using Office 365, some situations will surely arise in which you have to seek possible or likely solutions to some problems. While some problems are solvable, there are some you may need to seek the help of professionals and experts.

The common problems experienced by Office 365 users may include incorrect passwords, not having a recovery email, and so much more.

How to solve incorrect user ID or password

It can be frustrating when you try to sign in to your Office 365 portal and see a message that reads, **"we are unable to recognize this user ID or password"**. This incident normally happens when a user accidentally types in the wrong login information.

Here are the ways of solving this issue:

1. Check your ID

The first step to solving incorrect user IDs is to check that your ID is correctly entered and you are trying to sign in with the right email. For instance, the email usually used to sign in to office 365 looks like <u>someone@example.com</u>. Perhaps, if you are unsure about the User ID issued to you, try contacting your admin.

2. Check your Password

In some cases, workers save their passwords on their PCs and copy and page the data into sign-in boxes. However, this can result in problems, especially if you are entirely copying the password from another location. If that is the case, check for the spaces left at the start and end of the password.

Do not forget that some passwords are case sensitive, meaning that every letter in the upper case should be entered with the upper case.

Activating Office 365 without accessing the portal

Here's how to activate Office 365 without accessing the portal:

1. Configure Internet Explorer's Intranet Zone

Microsoft Office 365 uses different domains for several products and services. Also, the long list of domains must be included in Internet Explorer's intranet zone, which will serve as the default intranet settings, ensuring all cloud-based apps run while having the same configurations as internal apps.

2. Remove Old Office Licenses

Most times, Office 365 activation problems come up on desktops with an old software version. This also means that an outdated Office license can lead to activation problems and should be removed if you want to activate Office 365 without accessing the portal.

Usually, the tool to change and manage volume licenses is referred to as OSSP.vbs. This particular script can be found in the below directory:

C:\Program Files\Microsoft Office\OfficeXX.

If you are searching for an already present volume licenses utilizing a command prompt on your local system, you should run the below command;

cscript.exe "C:\Program Files (x86)\Microsoft

Office\Office16\ospp.vbs" /dstatus

Each license in the system is shown as a distinct block with full information. To delete the former licenses, you will have to find the final five digits of the product and run the below command:

cscript.exe "C:\Program Files (x86)\Microsoft

Office\Office16\ospp.vbs" /unpkey:TCK7R

Once you remove all the previous license keys for each product key, you can run the command again.

WORKING WITH SHORTCUTS ON PUBLISHER

Familiarize yourself with these shortcut keys to increase the pace and the speed at which you work on Publisher. You must commit them to memory to maximize the Publisher application and gain the most out of it.

SHORTCUTS KEYS ON PUBLISHER

SHORTCUT KEYS	FUNCTIONS
Ctrl + Shift + K	Change the Upper case to lower case
Ctrl + O	Access the Open Publication dialog box
Ctrl + F4	Close currently open publication
Ctrl + N	Open new publication
Ctrl + S	Access the Save dialog box to save your publication
Ctrl + F	Find specific information
Ctrl + H	Find a specific item and replace it with another item.
Ctrl + A	Select all the items on a page or all the text in a text frame.
Ctrl + U	Underline the selected text
Ctrl + B	Bold the selected text
Ctrl + I	Italicize the selected text
F7	Spelling checker
Shift + F7	Thesaurus task pane
Ctrl + Shift + F	Access Font dialog box
Ctrl + Shift+ C	Copy the formation on the text
Ctrl + Shift +	Paste the text formatting

	V
Ctrl + **Spacebar**	Change the character formatting to the style currently in use
Ctrl + Shift + **Y**	Switch On or Off the Special Character
Ctrl + Shift + **=**	Attach or detach Superscript formatting
Ctrl + =	Attach or detach Subscript formatting
Ctrl + Shift + **[**	Decrease the space between letters
Ctrl + Shift + **]**	Increase the space between the selected letters

GENERAL SHORTCUTS KEY ON PUBLISHER

SHORTCUT KEYS	FUNCTIONS
Ctrl + Shift + **>**	Increase the font size of the selected text
Ctrl + Shift + **<**	Decrease the font size of the selected text
Ctrl + L	Align the text to the left of the paragraph
Ctrl + R	Align the text to the right of the paragraph
Ctrl + E	Center align the text on a paragraph
Ctrl + J	Justify the text alignment on a paragraph
Ctrl +]	Increase the font size by 1 point
Ctrl + [	Decrease the font size by 1 point
Alt + Shift + **T**	Insert the recent time
Alt + Shift + **P**	Insert the current page number
Ctrl + Shift + **H**	Access the Hyphenation dialog box
Alt + Shift +	Insert the recent date

D	
Ctrl + Z	Undo the last action
Ctrl + Y	Redo the last action that you have undone
Ctrl + Shift + D	Share a paragraph consistently horizontally
Ctrl + Shift + J	Specify newspaper alignment
Alt + F6	take the object to the front
Alt + Shift + F6	Take the object to the back
Ctrl + Shift + G	Group the selected object/ungroup the selected object
Shift + R, F10	switch the snap to guides On and Off
Ctrl + Page down	Go to the next page
Ctrl + Page up	Go to the previous page
Ctrl + P	Access the Print dialog box
Ctrl + K	Insert Hyperlink
Ctrl + Shift + O	Switch boundaries On and Off
Ctrl + M	Switch between the Master page and the current page
Alt + F11	Access the Visual Basic Editor
Alt + F8	Access the Macros dialog box

Book 9: - OneDrive

Think of OneDrive as a secure Microsoft PC where you can upload anything. You will recognize that when we refer to a "cloud," we refer to objects thousands of miles above the land. In light of that, it was constructed with great security for the documents kept inside. In contrast to malware attacks on flash drive storage, it is difficult for files kept in OneDrive to become corrupt.

On the other hand, when you first sign up with OneDrive, a folder is automatically generated. The personal vault is the name of this Folder. The Folder is more secure than usual. It's advised that you keep your private documents in this Folder. Your tax information, driver's license, identity cards, and, if you like, any documents, including passwords, should all be saved in this Folder. OneDrive also functions on Mac computers, Android phones, iOS phones, Windows phones, and Windows phones (apple phones). If you use any of these devices, you can install the program on them, and it will function properly.

The OneDrive program likely comes pre-installed on your Windows PC if it runs Windows 10 or later. To search for OneDrive, all you have to do is click on your computer's start button, type OneDrive into the search bar, and then sign up or sign in if you currently use a Microsoft application on your phone or computer. OneDrive will then begin operating actively on your PC. But I'll walk you through the process step by step.

Additionally, even if your computer runs an outdated version of Windows, such as Windows 7, the OneDrive application will still function properly. You must visit the OneDrive website at http://OneDrive   .com/download as your initial step. You will be taken to the website's download page, and the page is depicted in the image below.

About to start the OneDrive   for PC download

To download the OneDrive software to your computer, select the download option. You must complete further steps for the program to be installed and enabled on your computer. Find the PC folder where the application was downloaded first. It should be in your computer's download folder by default. Double-click the downloaded software when you first see it. If you wish the application to make changes to your computer, your computer will ask you before you click the next button. Up until you hit the finish button, keep pressing the next button.

You will notice a notification on it as soon as the installation is complete. Then locate the OneDrive program you just installed and choose it by clicking the start button on your computer. Type your email address and sign in if you've previously created a Microsoft account. However, if you have never had a Microsoft account, simply select Create Account and proceed with the other guide. A OneDrive folder is automatically created on your computer after you create the account or sign in.

Establishing a OneDrive account

You must register a Microsoft account to use the OneDrive software fully. If you already use any Microsoft services on your computer or phone, you must already have an account with Microsoft. Microsoft Office, Microsoft Outlook, and Skype are a few examples of the Microsoft services I'm referring to, and these are all Microsoft-developed goods.

Because you automatically created a Microsoft account when setting up your OneDrive account, I'll assume in this section that you didn't have one previously. You only have an email address that you've been using. You may have generated this email address with Google (Gmail), Yahoo (yahoo mail), or Apple (iCloud mail).

Ensure your computer is properly connected to the internet before starting the setup. Wi-Fi or mobile data can be used to connect to the internet. I assume you've previously set up the OneDrive software on your PC at this point. But if you haven't, you can get it from the website at http://OneDrive .com/download and install it on your computer using the instructions I provided in the last three sentences of the subheading. But the program came pre-installed if your PC runs Windows 10 or higher. Therefore, there is no need for you to download and install it.

Type "OneDrive " into the search bar after selecting the start button on your computer. What I want you to do is described in the photo below.

The first step to set up a OneDrive account

As you type the word OneDrive, the OneDrive software will be displayed as one of the applications installed on your computer. Click the application for it to open and see it appear, as shown in the photo below.

What you will see as the desktop application opens

The next step you need to take is to click create an account. This will take you to the online page where you can start filling in the necessary information for the OneDrive account to be created for you. You will be required to select a language you understand. I assume you understand the English language, so select English. This will open the webpage fully; you will see this page below.

The OneDrive webpage for account creating

The next step you need to take is to click the link to see plans and pricing as indicated on the page above. This will open a new webpage that shows the plans and pricing of different Microsoft 365 packages, as shown in the photo below.

The Microsoft 365 plans and pricing with that of OneDrive

From the above, there are some options. If you want to create OneDrive for your business, click the for business heading. But I assume you are an individual who wants to create a OneDrive account for your personal use. I select the for-home option, which shows the plans and pricing.

You may wonder why you see Microsoft 365 family and Microsoft 365 personal options among the subscription plans instead of just OneDrive standalone and OneDrive basic. The reason for that is that when you buy a Microsoft 365 subscription, you have OneDrive software as one of the applications in the office suite. With this, you will have word 365, access 365, PowerPoint 365, excel 365, publisher 365, and OneDrive applications installed on your computer.

But, if your interest is just in the OneDrive software, you must choose OneDrive standalone or OneDrive basic. For this learning, I will go with the OneDrive basic, free. So, click the link and signup for free under the OneDrive basic plan. This will open a new page which I show in the photo below.

Progress in creating a OneDrive account

There is space for you to enter the email address you want to use to sign up for the account. You must click the place that has **some@example.com** and type your email address. Click the next button for a new page to open. The next page you will see is shown in the photo below.

Enter the password you want to use to be signed in

Create your password in the space written to create a password. As you type the password, your web browser may suggest a strong password. You may click the suggested password or reject it. But in most cases, I prefer creating my password by myself instead of the one suggested by the browser. I prefer creating my password because I can easily remember it. You can tick the checkbox at show password to see the password you entered and be sure everything is correct. Click the next button for you to continue your account setup.

Fill in your first and last names

The above photo shows the next page you will be taken to. You are required to fill in your first name and last names correctly. After filling in the names, click the next button.

The next page is the page for entering your country and date of birth information. The photo I have below shows the page.

The ellipsis indicated in the photo

As the ellipsis is tapped, select save, which is one of the options that you will see.

Tap the save button

As you tap the save button, the file becomes saved on your phone within a short time.

How to make your OneDrive file available offline

It is possible to make any file you have on your OneDrive account to be available offline. Offline files can easily be accessed even when your mobile phone is not connected to the internet.

To make a file in your OneDrive account available offline, as your phone is connected to the internet, tap the OneDrive mobile application for it to open. Tap the files tab to see the files and folders in your account.

Locate the file you want to have offline, and press and hold the file for it to be selected. The photo below shows my selected file, which I want to make available offline.

Select a file to be made available offline

Tap the ellipsis (the three dots) at the top right of the screen.

Some of the options after the ellipsis is tapped

From the options that you will see, select make available offline. On taking action, the selected file is made available offline.

Changing how to update your offline files

In most situations, updating offline files is put over wi-fi, but it can be changed to another option. You can set it in your OneDrive mobile application that offline files should be updated via mobile data. These are the steps you need to take to get it done.

Tap your OneDrive mobile application for it to open. Make sure your phone is connected to the internet.

The next step is to tap the me tab, which is indicated in the photo below.

Me tab, among other basic OneDrive mobile tabs

As you tap me tab, you will see some buttons you can click to achieve a particular task. Out of them, tap the settings button.

Directly under the options heading, tap the part that reads update offline files.

And lastly, select the option wi-fi and mobile data. The options are displayed in the photo below

Selecting the option on how to update offline files

Files sharing on OneDrive mobile app

Irrespective of how I walked you through how you can share files on the OneDrive website, you can still share files through the mobile application when you log into the site.

To share any file, tap your OneDrive mobile application for it to open. Tap the files tab on your OneDrive account. You will see some files you have in your account. Select the file you want to share with others by long-press and hold.

You will see the share icon on top of the screen. Just tap the share icon. The screenshot below shows the position of the share icon on top of your OneDrive mobile application.

The share icon indicated

As you tap this share icon, you will see channels through which you can share the selected file. The photo below shows that when I tapped the icon.

The share options on OneDrive mobile app

If you choose send files (sending the file you selected as an attachment), you are to send the file through any file-sharing applications on your phone. In most cases, I like sending to people's email addresses. So, I will select Gmail concerning that. Spaces will be provided for me to type the email addresses of my recipients, and I will then type them and hit send button.

On the other hand, you can decide to send links to people. When you send links, the recipients receiving the links can tap it to view the link's main content, which is your file in this case.

To send as a link, select the file you want to share and tap the share icon. From the shared medium that you will see, click the copy link. This is indicated in the photo below.

The copy link share media indicated

As you do this, the link is copied to your device clipboard. With this, you can send the link to different people you want. If you want to share through messenger, send the links to their inboxes by pasting the link first and then sending it. If you want to send the link to recipients' email addresses, log into your email address, type them in the space provided, and then paste the link on the body of the mail before taping the send button. The recipients will get the links in their email address inboxes quickly.

There are many ways of sharing files on your OneDrive account through a mobile application. You can easily share through Bluetooth, Instagram, Facebook, direct to the browser, and many more. Feel free to experiment with all the channels you see when you tap the share icon. By experimenting with the channels, you will become a pro. And experience is the best teacher.

Moving files to a new Folder on OneDrive   mobile app

You can move files from one location to another in your account using the mobile application. Maybe the file is not in any folder, and you want it placed in a folder you created. It is possible to do that.

To achieve that, tap your mobile application to open. Tap your files tab to see the files you have on your OneDrive account. If the file you want to move to another folder already exists in a folder, tap the Folder it exists in for it to open.

Select the file by long pressing on the file. As it is selected, tap the move icon at the screen's top part. The move icon is indicated in the photo below.

The move icon **you are to tap**

As you tap the move icon, the folders existing in your account are displayed. Select the Folder you want the file moved into, and tap the move here button. As you take this last bold step, the file is moved to the selected Folder.

To add to your knowledge, you can create a new folder immediately and move your file in it as you click the move icon. To get that done, tap the + sign in the rectangle folder icon, as shown in the photo below.

Creating a new folder to move a file in it

As you tap that icon, type the name you want the Folder to bear and hit create button. And lastly, tap the move here button, which appears at the bottom. Immediately, your file is moved to the new Folder you just created.

Book 10: - SharePoint

SharePoint can be accessed online or via the on-premises option. With this analysis, you can decide which SharePoint best suits your organization's activities using the SharePoint online Microsoft 365 or the on-premises SharePoint of 2013, 2016, 2019, and others.

Firstly, if you are a new subscriber to SharePoint online, Microsoft is providing a truckload of benefits in the new SharePoint Online. However, some organizations are still over completely to the SharePoint online space. Some of these people felt insecure about the cloud as it could also be exposed to cyber insecurities. Others feel the working techniques in SharePoint will be too different from the SharePoint online.

With SharePoint on-premises, you would need to manually activate some functions and pay a fee for licensing the software. An IT team has to be on standby to make adjustments when necessary. With this, scalability becomes difficult and can be very expensive to maintain. But, the Microsoft cloud version is maintained by the Microsoft team without any maintenance headache associated with on-premises servers.

Also, SharePoint online is easy to use through a token subscription fee that can be paid monthly or yearly, depending on your preference. Your choice of subscription plan can be influenced based on the nature of your business.

Moreso, your SharePoint online can be used via omnichannel. You can commence a SharePoint process on your mobile phone and conclude it on your laptop from another location. All this process requires is a good source of internet connection. By doing this, you can easily access your Microsoft Word, OneDrive, Outlook, and any other application when the need arises without tampering with your SharePoint activities.

For security, your information in SharePoint is stored in the Microsoft data center or cloud. The Microsoft cloud has the highest number of specific industry-standard securities, which makes your information secure.

Data migration from the premises to the online space can be easily done for an organization that already used the SharePoint on-premises version. Although some functionalities defer, you will still be able to use the SPF X development to rectify this difference.

Moreso, with the new SharePoint Online, several features are already automated by its manufacturers, making the job of the user much easier. With the on-premises SharePoint, if your user base increases, you need to add additional servers that cost a fortune. On the other hand, with SharePoint Online, you take additional licenses for the new users.

In a nutshell, either version of SharePoint is good software. You can decide to use either or both depending on the best-suited preference for your business.

How to Identify your Version of SharePoint

Knowing what version of SharePoint you are using can help you receive the best outcomes and support for any element of your SharePoint; therefore, it is crucial.

To know the version, you are using;

- Open your SharePoint and at the top right side, click on the **question mark(?) sign** which stands for "help".

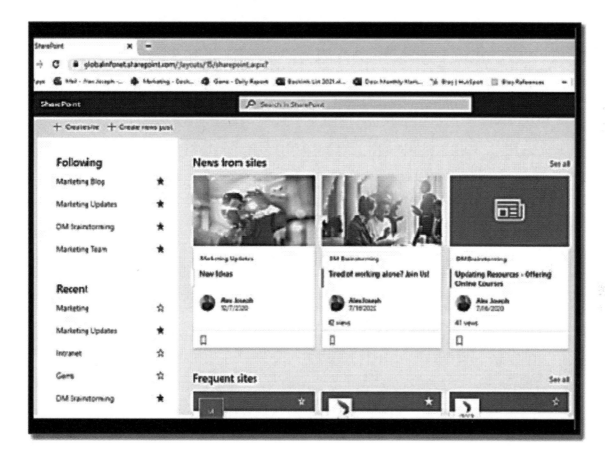

- Using SharePoint Online, your help panel will look like the image below.

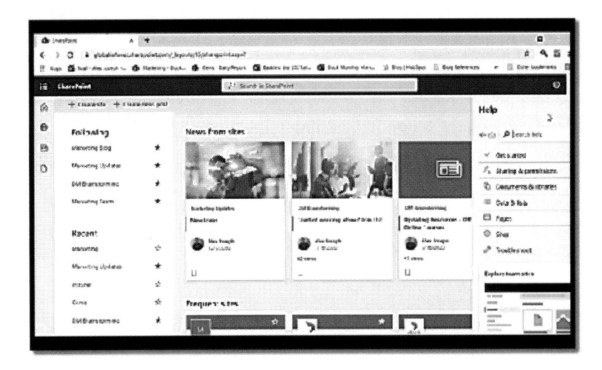

If you use an older version, the version's name will be written beside the **Help** option in the help panel.

After knowing your version, click on the **search bar** to find the kind of solution you need.

Benefits of the SharePoint Online

As explained earlier, SharePoint online has several benefits.

Its usefulness to an individual, a group of people, or an organization is inexhaustible. Some of these benefits include;

- It easily grants external access to files, folders, and websites.

- Using OneDrive within SharePoint online gives users freedom from the network from a network share.

- The new SharePoint online gets updated frequently by Microsoft. New and better features are added regularly, giving users a unique user experience at intervals.

- It can be used on an omnichannel; this removes any limiting barrier to a single device for use.

- You can easily upgrade or downgrade your SharePoint online by subscribing to a plan.

- Also, the cost of human resources is reduced drastically while using SharePoint online, as most features are automated.

122

- Its security measures include tight multiple authentication factors and enterprise-grade security to protect its users against negative penetrations in the cloud.

- It meets industry-specific compliance standards like HIPAA, FISMA, and ISO 27001.

SharePoint online is a good choice to add to your software collection.

Data Center and Hardware

Have you ever wondered where your command travels to anytime you do a google search or use the Google Assistant for a question? Your commands travel through several seas, underground forests, climbs through mountains, and beyond valleys to a place where the many data in the world converge. This is called the **Data Center.**

The data center is an infrastructure or building that houses powerful computers used to run a company's services. Here, information is processed, and data is stored, managed, and disseminated across these computers. Alongside this, network infrastructures will be established to support other virtual needs of the device.

In modern times, many companies depend on Google Cloud to provide them with data center functions, which help to process big data and serve millions of users.

For SharePoint, data is stored in the Microsoft Cloud space. There is a free OneDrive space where you can easily store data from your SharePoint.

To create your first SharePoint site, you need to have an Office 365 account for business.

The first step in using Microsoft Forms is to Login into the Microsoft account using your registered **Username** and **Password**.

To Access Microsoft SharePoint

- Go to the Application Launcher located on the top-left of the **Microsoft 365** page.

- Select **SharePoint** from the list of applications.

- **Microsoft SharePoint** web app will open.

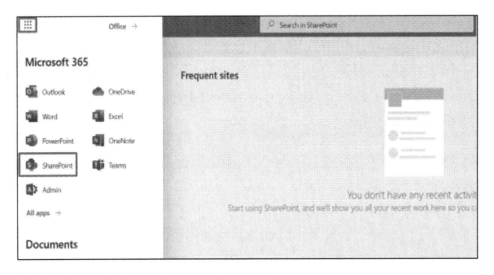

NAVIGATING THE HOME PAGE

When you are just starting as a new user of the SharePoint site, a screen appears as shown below;

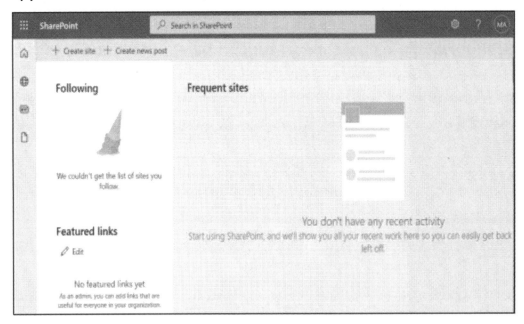

Frequent: This shows items you or other team members have worked on.

Featured links: This is where the administration can bring out important links to areas of the site people might need.

CREATING A NEW SITE

Information is available on SharePoint. Different kinds of content or web elements are stored and arranged on websites. Similar to the rooms in your home, each of these places has a certain function. A site may be a communication site or a team site.

A team site is used to coordinate tasks, keep track of events, communicate with your team, and share documents.

A communication site's purpose is to disseminate information to a wide audience, with a small number of members providing the data that the vast audience uses.

Contents of a SharePoint site

A SharePoint team site offers many features. You'll find the following contents to be important:

- **Lists**

Five pre-built lists are available on a SharePoint team site: announcements, contacts, events, tasks, and links. You can add features to these links and change their appearance, and Microsoft Excel spreadsheets can be imported into the lists to use their data.

- **Document Libraries**

Team members can exchange files using this module. Documents may be generated, updated, managed, and shared from a single location.

- **Discussion Boards**

Due to the decrease in frequent emails between members, it is crucial. Threads are developed for various objectives so that prior conversations can be readily tracked and traced without too much effort.

- **Surveys**

You can use these to make member surveys to get their feedback rapidly.

Create a new team site

A team site gives you and your team a place to collaborate on projects while working remotely. Web pages, file document libraries, lists, and web sections are all included.

A team site involves cooperating with other people on a certain task as team members. When using a team site, all participants must contribute to and share the site's contents, and the audience is only the members and any other connected individuals.

To create a team site

- Go to the top of the SharePoint page.
- Click **+ Create site.**

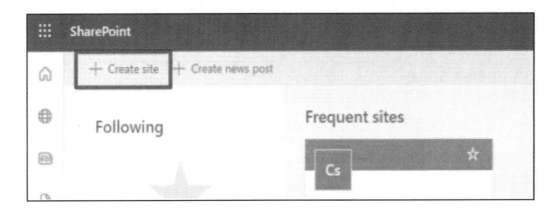

- Choose **Team site.** The team site wizard will be launched for you to input your site information.

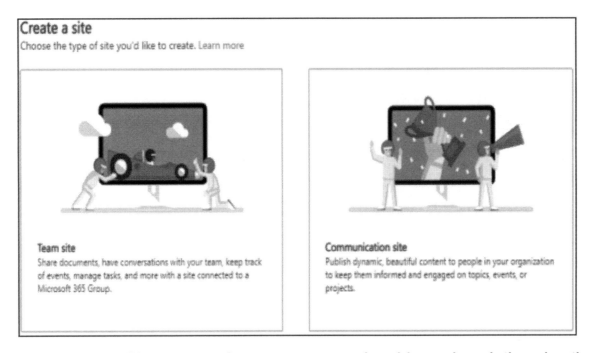

- Give your site a **name** and add a description in the **Site description** box that describes its purpose. A group email address and Site address will be generated to edit.

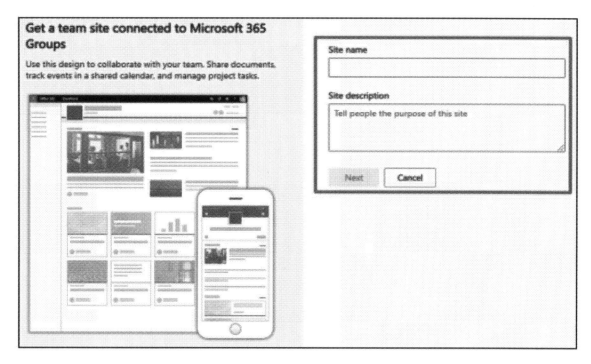

- Go to the **Privacy Settings** to make the team site either **Public** so that anyone can access it or **Private** only members can have access to it.

- Choose your preferred language in the **Select a language** box.

- Click **Next**.

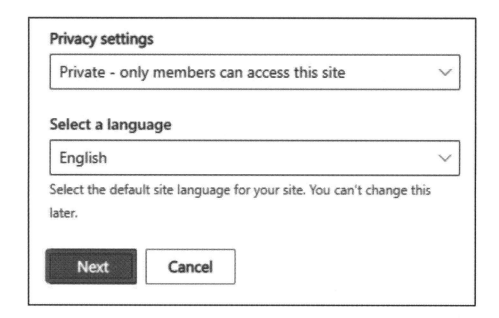

- In the **additional add owners,** add the name or email of those who will serve as co-owners.

- In the **Add members** column, add the names or emails of everyone you want to be a member of your site. You can still add members later, even after creating.
- Click **Finish** when you are done.

Team site home page

Several items can be found on the Microsoft SharePoint Homepage are;

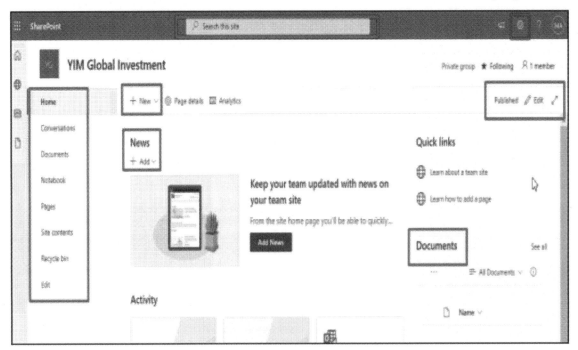

- **New** – This button allows you to create a new list, document library, page, etc.

- **Add** – To create a news post news link.

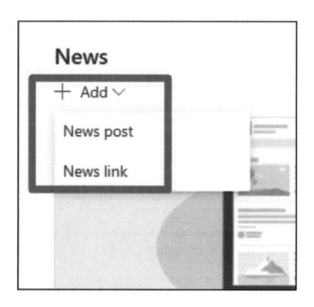

- **News** – This shows the latest happenings with your team, e.g., news, information, updates, etc.
- **Documents** – This displays items from the default document library. Drag and drop is a method for adding documents.
- **Activity** – This allows you to see other people's movements at a glance when they add or edit files, pages, or lists.

- **Settings** – Here, you can change the look of the team site, including the theme and header.

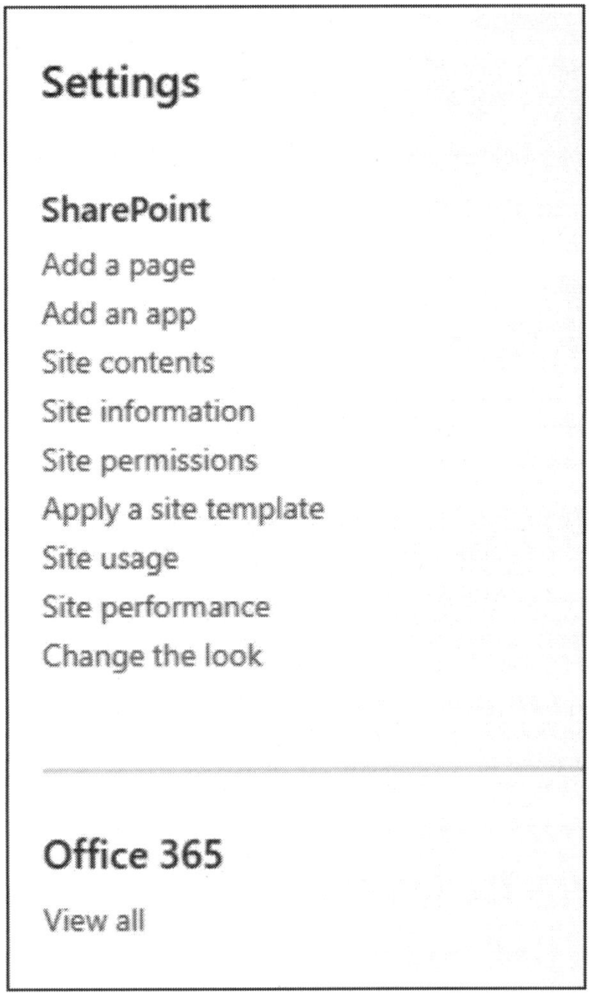

Settings

SharePoint

Add a page

Add an app

Site contents

Site information

Site permissions

Apply a site template

Site usage

Site performance

Change the look

Office 365

View all

- **Search** – This is where you can type the name of files to search for on the team site.

- **Site Contents** – This is used to manage your sites.

- **Documents** - This is a default document library for your team. Your store and share files on documents.

- **Edit** – This is used for moving different navigation sites up and down.

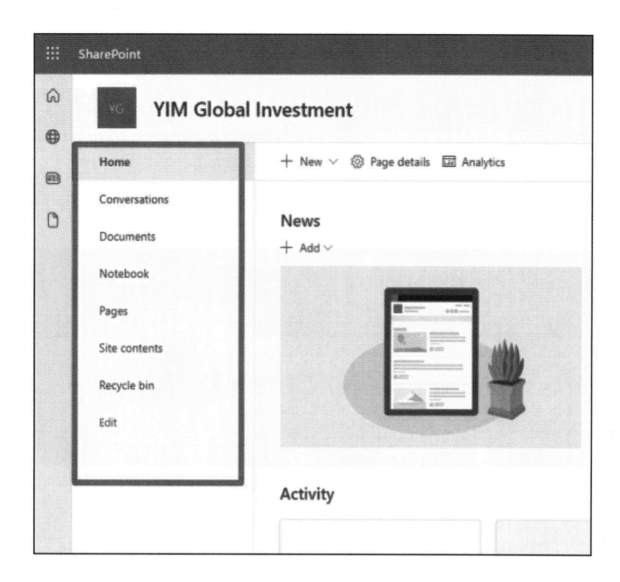

Creating and Uploading files

To create a file

- Click **Documents.**
- Go to **New** and select the file type you want.
- The new file will open. You add the information you want and make the necessary changes to it. Your new file will be automatically saved to your document library.

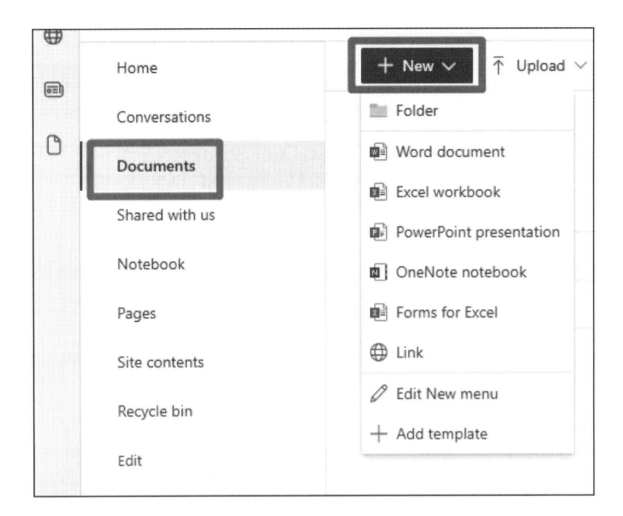

To rename a file

- Click the down arrow to the left of the **saved.**

- Give the file a different name in the name box.

- Click the team site name to see the new file in your document library.

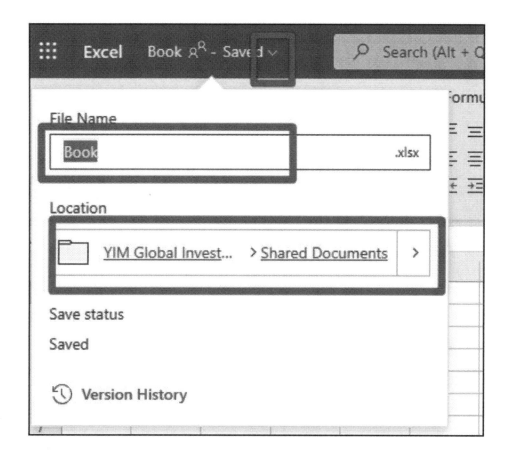

To upload a file

- The drag-and-drop method is the easiest way to upload files to a SharePoint document library.

- Open the location of your file, drag and drop it into the document library it will be uploaded.

Alternatively;

- Go to the **Documents library**.

- Click **Uploads**.

- Select whether you want to upload files, folders, or Templates.

- Choose the file, folder, or template from its location.

- It will be uploaded to your document library.

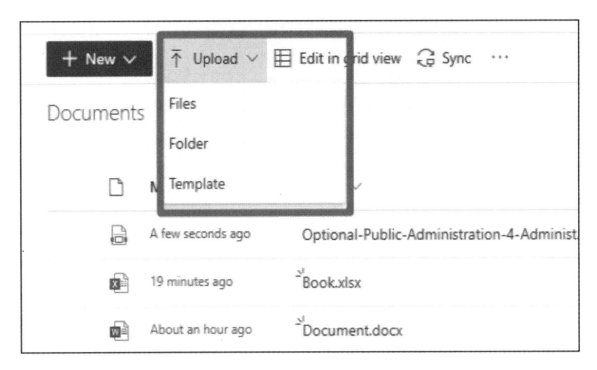

To share a file

- Please select the file you want to share by clicking on its extreme left.

- Select **Share.**

- Select whether to add the names of the people you want to share the file with or **Copy the Link** to create a link to the file that you can share in an email.

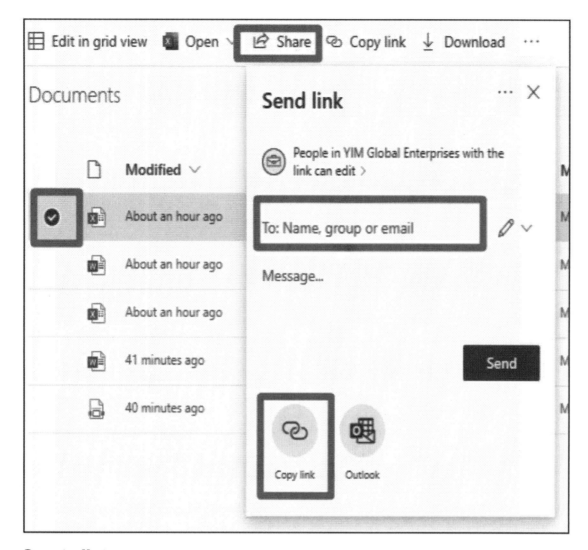

Create list

A list is created to keep track of information, people, dates, etc. A list can be made from an Excel spreadsheet, an existing list, or predesigned templates of Microsoft 365.

To create a list

- Go to **New.**
- Select **List** from the drop-down menu.

- Select from the list of options you want to create

- **Blank:** This makes you create a list from scratch and give it a Name, Description (Optional), and any other options.

- **From Excel:** This creates a list based on an Excel spreadsheet.

- **From existing list:** This creates a list based on the columns in another list. Your new list will not contain any data from the original list but will start with the same columns.

- **Templates:** This allows you to select a predesigned template and create your list.

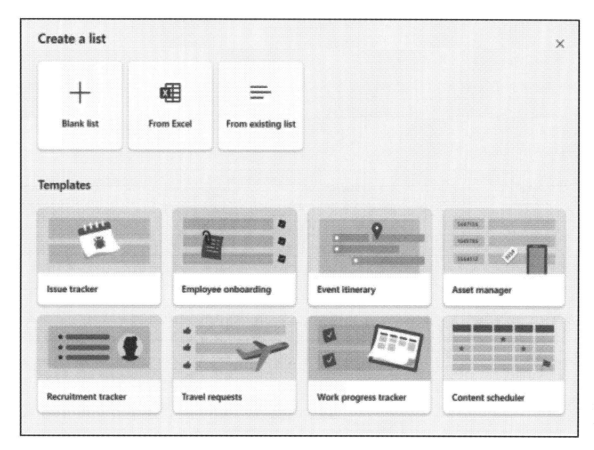

- After naming your list and describing it, click **Create.** Your new list opens.

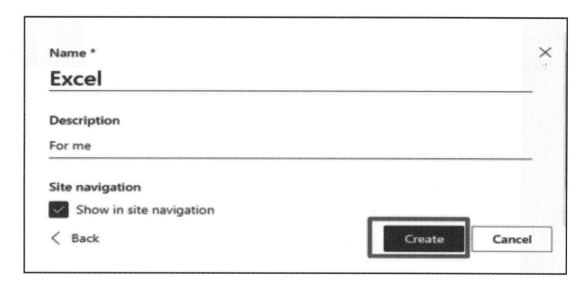

- Click **Add column** and select the type of information to add to the list.

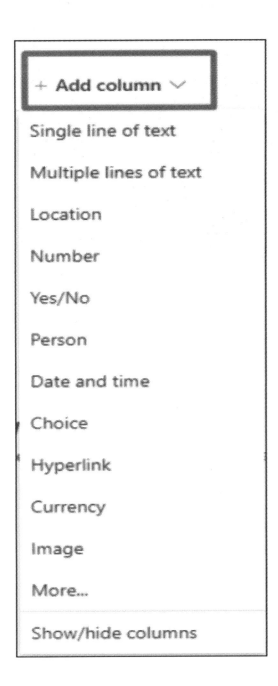

How to delete a web part

If you are not satisfied with a particular web part, you can choose to delete it by following the steps below:

1. Click Edit your area in the top right corner if it is not currently in edit mode.

2. Select the web section you want to get rid of.

3. Click the **trash can icon** or press the **Delete key** on your keyboard.

4. Select **Yes** to confirm your deletion.

How to edit a page after the first configuration

You may see and modify a page's properties in the Page details window. You can change the image, add a description, and designate a page to a particular category, among other things. Also, you could build custom attributes for pages.

Notes: Organizations that have opted into the Targeted release program will progressively get certain capabilities. This means you may not see this feature yet, or it may appear differently than stated in the help pages.

The amount of properties accessible to see and modify on a page varies based on the properties given to it by the item owner or your administrator. Some of these characteristics may be necessary.

Edit and see the page's properties

To see the page's properties, go to:

- On a saved or published page, click **Page information** at the top of the page in read-only mode.

- Click More details at the window's bottom for more information about a page (such as the latest updated date).

To modify the page's properties, go to:

- Select Page details from the command bar.

NB: You must have owner or designer rights on the SharePoint site to change the page properties. Select Settings > Site permissions and then Site Owners to see who owns the site.

- Select **Edit** from the command bar to the left of the Page details window.

- Pick Properties in the Page details pane, and then select the property's value beneath the property name you wish to modify.

- To save your changes, type the new value and then click Enter.

- To modify several settings, choose Edit all, then edit the properties you wish to alter before clicking **Save**.

- To publish your modifications, choose **Republish**.

Alternatively, you may choose **Discard changes** on the command bar to reverse your modifications.

How to add individual content items

Contacts, calendars, announcements, and problem tracking are just some of the list elements that can be included in a list. You may also put the following things on your list: Columns have Text, Number, Choice, Currency, Date and Time, Lookup, Yes/No, and Calculated.

Lists may be created in Microsoft SharePoint, Microsoft 365's Lists app, or Microsoft Teams. You could attach files to a list item to offer extra details, such as a spreadsheet with supporting statistics or a paper with background information.

Note: You must have edit rights to add, modify, or remove list items. *NB: Contact your SharePoint administrator if you don't see any choices to add or modify list items.*

1. Go to the website for the list to which you wish to add an item.
2. To access the **New item window**, click the + New or + New item. Note that the look and navigation of a site may be substantially altered. Contact your administrator if you can't find an option, such as a command, button, or link.
3. *Fill in the details for the list item. **Note: Data must be entered into a column (field) marked with an asterisk *.***

To attach files to a list item, choose Add attachments in the New item box, then pick the file. When selecting files, hold down the CTRL key to attach several files.

Select OK after selecting **Open**. Your list doesn't allow attachments if the Add attachments function isn't accessible.

4. *Click the **Save button**.*

How to change the layout

After you've signed in and updated a page, you may alter the Page Layout (either pick Edit Page from the Site Actions dropdown menu or click the Edit button).

1. Click the Page tab on the ribbon, then the Page Layout dropdown.

2. Choose your preferred layout and wait for the page to refresh.

NB: Don't forget to Save & Close and Check In once you've finished updating the page.

Final Words

Microsoft Office 365's most recent features are available to you immediately so that you can have the newest technology at a lower cost and in less time than if you tried to keep your computer up-to-date. The new features are available in the latest versions of Word, Excel, PowerPoint, and Outlook. You can also use them on Mac computers or mobile devices running iOS or Android. You can use Office 365 in various ways, including at work and at home. You can also use it with your school or organization's account to access and share documents with others in your group. I hope this book has helped you understand what Office 365 is and how it can benefit you or your organization. I hope the book also gives ideas about what technology solutions might work for your business or organization. I sincerely hope that you have found this book to be helpful. If so, please consider leaving a review on Amazon or Goodreads. Thanks!